THE LIFE
OF
JESUS

SUPPOSE THAT CHRIST HAD NOT BEEN BORN

Suppose that Christ had not been born
That faraway Judean morn!

Suppose that God, whose mighty hand
Created worlds, had never planned

A way for man to be redeemed.
Suppose the Wise Men only dreamed

That guiding star whose light still glows
Down through the centuries. Suppose

Christ never walked here in man's sight,
Our blessed Way, and Truth, and Light.

Suppose He counted all the cost,
And never cared that we were lost,

And never died for you and me,
Nor shed His blood on Calvary

Upon a shameful cross. Suppose
That having died, He never rose,

And there was none with power to save
Our souls from death beyond the grave!

O faraway Judean morn—
Suppose that Christ had not been born!

"Thanks be unto God for His unspeakable gift!"

–MARTHA SNELL NICHOLSON

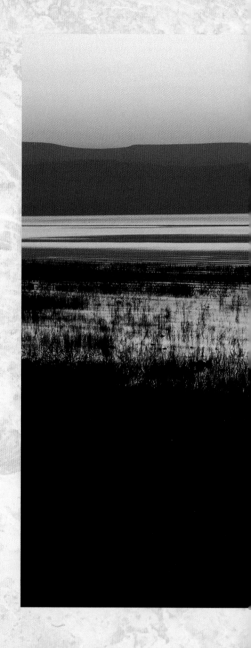

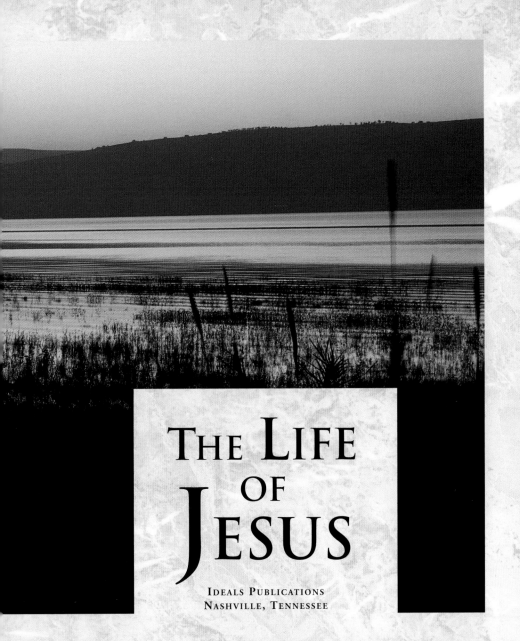

The Life of Jesus

Ideals Publications
Nashville, Tennessee

ISBN 0-8249-4303-1

Published by Ideals Publications, a division of Guideposts
535 Metroplex Drive, Suite 250
Nashville, Tennessee 37211
www.idealsbooks.com

Printed and bound in Italy

Library of Congress CIP data on file

10 9 8 7 6 5 4 3 2

Front cover photo: Sunset at Ruby Beach, Olympic National Park, Washington (copyright © by Dennis Frates).

Photo, page 2: The Lake of Gennesaret, more commonly known as the Sea of Galilee (Erich Lessing/Art Resource). *Photo, opposite page: Jaffa Gate in the Old City section of Jerusalem* (George Hunter/H. Armstrong Roberts). *Photo, pages 6–7: Caves at Qumran where the Dead Sea Scrolls were found—including a complete manuscript of the Book of Isaiah with its many prophecies* (Jeanne Conte).

Photograph on page 137 courtesy of the National Shrine of Our Lady of Lourdes, 21281 Chardon Road, Cleveland, OH 44117.

ACKNOWLEDGMENTS

BARCLAY, WILLIAM. "Thomas Believes" from *The Master's Men.* Copyright © 1959 by William Barclay. Published by Abingdon Press. Originally published by SCM Press Ltd., London. Used by permission of SCM-Canterbury Press Ltd. BISHOP, JIM. "God Sends an Angel" and "In the Garden" from *The Day Christ Was Born.* Copyright © 1959 by Jim Bishop. HarperCollins Publishers. BONSER, EDNA MADISON. "The Question the Wise Men Asked" and "The Good That Grew in Nazareth" from *The Little Boy of Nazareth* by Edna Madison Bonser. Copyright © 1930 by Harper & Bros. and renewed 1958 by Virginia Bonser Brooks. BORG, MARCUS. "The Miracles of Jesus" from *Jesus, A New Vision.* Copyright © 1987 by Marcus Borg. HarperCollins Publishers. BROUWER, SIGMUND. "The Sign on the Cross" from *The Carpenter's Cloth.* Copyright © 1997 by Sigmund Brouwer. Used by permission of W Publishing Group, Nashville, TN. BUCK, PEARL S. "Jesus in the Synagogue" from *The Story Bible.* Copyright © 1971 by Pearl S. Buck and Lyle Kenyon Engel. Used by permission of Harold Ober Associates, Inc. CROWELL, GRACE NOLL. "Jesus Feeds the Multitude" and "The Master Teacher" from *Come See a Man.* Copyright © 1956 by Abingdon Press. Used by permission of Abingdon Press. DANIEL-ROPS, HENRI. "Peter and the Glory of God" and "A Portrait of Jesus" from *Jesus and His Times* by Henri Daniel-Rops, translated by Ruth Millar. Copyright © 1954, 1956 by E.P. Dutton. Used by permission of Dutton, a division of Penguin Putnam, Inc. and by Librairie Arthéme Fayard, Paris. FERRARI, ERMA. "His Faithful Followers" and "Tidings of Great Joy" from *The Life of Jesus of Nazareth* by Erma Ferrari. Copyright © 1958 by Simon & Schuster. GIBRAN, KAHLIL. "Simon the Cyrene" from *Jesus, The Son of Man.* Copyright © 1928 by Kahlil Gibran and renewed 1956 by Administrators C.T.A. of Kahlil Gibran Estate and Mary G. Gibran. Used by permission of Alfred A. Knopf, a division of Random House, Inc. GOODSPEED, EDGAR J. "The End of a Prophet" from *A Life of Jesus* by Edgar J. Goodspeed. Copyright © 1950 by Harper & Bros. HarperCollins Publishers. GOUDGE, ELIZABETH. "Jesus Raises Lazarus" and "A Prophecy of Many Names" from *God So Loved the World.* Copyright © 1951 and renewed 1979 by Elizabeth Goudge. Used by permission of Harold Ober Associates, Inc. HOLMES, MARJORIE. "This Is My Beloved Son" and "Even the Winds and Sea Obey" from *The Messiah.* Copyright © 1987 by Marjorie Holmes. Published by Harper & Row. "Miracles Such As the World Has Never Seen" from *Three From Galilee.* Copyright © 1985 by Marjorie Holmes. Published by Harper & Row. KIRKLAND, WINIFRED. "Jesus in His Family" from *Discovering the Boy of Nazareth* by Winifred Kirkland. Published by MacMillan. KOMROFF, MANUEL. "One Who Came to Bring Life" from *In the Years of Our Lord.* Copyright © 1942 by Manuel Komroff. Published by Harper & Bros. MARSHALL, PETER. "Mary Magdalene Meets the Risen Lord" and "The Interview" from *The First Easter* by Peter Marshall. Copyright © 1959 by Catherine Marshall, renewed 1987 by Leonard E. LeSourd. Used by permission of Baker Book House. NAZHIVIN, IVAN. "On the Eve of the First Miracle" from *According to Thomas.* Translated by Emile Burns. Copyright © 1930 and renewed 1958 by Harper & Bros. OURSLER, FULTON. "The Chosen," "Jesus Banishes the Tempter," "The Long Journey," and "The Betrayal" from *The Greatest Story Ever Told.* Copyright © 1949 by Fulton Oursler. Published by Image Books, a division of Doubleday. OXENHAM, JOHN. "The Cross at the Crossways" from *Gentlemen, The King!* (Boston and Chicago: The Pilgrim Press, 1928). Used by permission. PEALE, NORMAN VINCENT. "The Last Supper," "The Cleansing of the Temple," and "Two Brothers from Capernaum" from *Jesus of Nazareth.* Copyright © 1966 by Ruth Stafford Peale, Margaret Peale Everett, Dr. John Stafford Peale, and Elizabeth Peale Allen. Reprinted by permission. POTEAT, EDWIN MCNEILL. "Leaving His Nazareth Home" from *These Shared His Cross.* Copyright © 1940, 1941 and 1948 by Harper & Bros. SANDBURG, CARL. "Child" from *Chicago Poems* by Carl Sandburg. Copyright © 1994 by Dover Publications, Inc. SHEEN, FULTON J. "Feed My Sheep," "More Than a Teacher," and "A Lesson of Forgiveness" from *The Life of Christ.* Copyright © 1958 and 1977 by Fulton J. Sheen. Published by Image Books, a division of Doubleday. SHINN, ROGER L. "The Lord's Prayer" from *The Sermon on the Mount* by Roger L. Shinn. (Philadelphia and Boston: United Church Press, 1954, 1961), 50-54. Adapted by permission. SPENCER, BONNELL. "Preaching the Gospel" and "An Empty Tomb" from *They Saw the Lord.* Copyright © 1983 by Bonnell Spencer. Used by permission of Morehouse Publishing, Harrisburg, PA. STEINMANN, JEAN. "Jesus Is Baptized" from *The Life of Jesus* by Jean Steinmann. Copyright © 1963 by Little, Brown and Co., Inc. (English translation), and used by their permission. Our sincere thanks to the following authors whom we were unable to locate: Steve Case for "The Light to Every Nation"; Allen Eastman Cross for "The Hidden Years"; Alice M. Darton for "The First Shadow Falls"; John Erskine for "The Shepherd Speaks"; Molly Anderson Haley for "Miracles"; Thomas S. Jones Jr. for "According to Saint Mark"; Mary King for "Mary of Bethlehem"; Brother Francis Patrick, F.S.C. for "Their Messiah Rejected"; Dallas Lore Sharp for "The Wise Men" and "Words of Meaning"; Edward Shillito for "Prayer of a Modern Thomas."

All possible care has been taken to fully acknowledge the ownership and use of every selection in this book. If any mistakes or omissions have occurred, they will be corrected in subsequent editions, provided notification is sent to the publisher.

CONTENTS

I

THE STORY UNFOLDS

And there shall come forth a

rod out of the stem of Jesse, and

a Branch shall grow out of His

roots: And the spirit of the LORD

shall rest upon Him, the spirit of

wisdom and understanding, the

spirit of counsel and might, the

spirit of knowledge and of the

fear of the LORD.

–ISAIAH 11:1–2

> But thou, Bethlehem Ephratah,
> though thou be little among the
> thousands of Judah, yet out of
> thee shall He come forth unto Me
> that is to be ruler in Israel; whose
> goings forth have been from of
> old, from everlasting.
>
> –MICAH 5:2

THE AGELESS CHRIST

Christ of the council chamber,
    Christ of the ageless past;
Christ of the prophet's vision,
    Christ that is first and last.

Christ of the lowly manger,
    Christ of the Virgin Birth;
Christ of the Wise Men and
    shepherds,
    Christ of the sin-cursed earth.

Christ of an infinite power,
    Christ of undisturbed poise;
Christ of a boundless love,
    Christ of eternal joys.

Christ of my dying hour,
    Christ of the other shore;
Christ as the ceaseless ages roll,
    He's my Christ forever more!

–B. L. BYER

A PROPHECY OF MANY NAMES

ELIZABETH GOUDGE

For centuries before He was born, they knew that He would come to them. Their prophets told them about Him, calling Him by many wonderful names: the Messiah, the Deliverer, the Holy One of Israel, the Son of Man. But most of them imagined He would come as a conqueror who would deliver His people from their earthly enemies and establish an earthly kingdom. Very few realized that the enemy He was coming to fight was man's selfishness, that He would conquer by suffering, and that His kingdom would be the spiritual kingdom of those who love God. Palestine—where the nomad people of Israel found a home at last—is a small country, and beautiful, but dry and mountainous and not very productive. And it is so wedged in between countries larger and wealthier than itself that throughout its history it has had little peace. Foreign armies have been perpetually marching across it, fighting battles on its soil, oppressing its people, or taking them into slavery. And it is this small and oppressed bit of country that the Creator of the whole immense universe called especially His own when He lived on earth.

The people of Israel enjoyed in their history a few short periods of freedom and prosperity, but God did not choose one of them in which to come among His people. Instead He chose a moment when they were having a difficult time. Rome had conquered nearly all of Europe, as well as Palestine. Many of the men in high places had made friends with the enemy for the sake of the comfort and security that this friendship brought them, but the rest of the nation was heavily taxed. They were not badly treated if they did what they were told, and the Romans were efficient rulers, but the people of Israel have always been a proud and independent

people. The loss of their freedom was bitter to them. The outward life of the country, the tending of the vineyards and olive groves, the plowing of the fields, the sowing and gathering of the crops, the lives of the farmers and shepherds and artisans and their families in the small villages perched upon the hilltops went on normally enough, but underneath it was much hidden anxiety and grief and pain, and into the middle of it all came God. And there was nothing of their life that He did not share with His people, and does not today share with us, because we are His people if we love Him, and He is as close to us as He was to them when they heard His voice and saw His face and put out their hand and touched Him. ✖

This spring landscape shows an almond tree blossoming near the Jordan River, a river of great significance in the New Testament. Much of Jesus' ministry took place in proximity to the river. (Geopress/H. Armstrong Roberts)

The Herald of the King

George Hodges

There was in the days of Herod, the king of Judaea, a certain priest named Zacharias, . . . and his wife . . . and her name was Elisabeth. And they had no child, because that Elisabeth was barren, and they both were now well stricken in years.

According to the custom of the priest's office, his lot was to burn incense when he went into the Temple of the Lord. And there appeared unto him an angel of the Lord standing on the right side of the altar of incense.

But the angel said unto him, Fear not, Zacharias: for thy prayer is heard; and thy wife Elisabeth shall bear thee a son, and thou shalt call his name John. And he shall go before him in the spirit and power of Elias, to turn the hearts of the fathers to the children, and the disobedient to the wisdom of the just; to make ready a people prepared for the Lord.

–Luke 1:5, 7, 9, 11, 13, 17

The King had long been expected. Men of God in the Old Testament had promised that the King should come. They had also promised that before He came, somebody should appear to tell the people that He was coming, and to prepare His way; for that was the custom when kings came.

At last, one day, just before the beginning of the Year One, a strange thing happened to a priest in the Temple. The priest was a very good old man named Zacharias. He lived with his good old wife, Elisabeth, in a quiet little place among the hills, where they were much respected and loved. Many times they had prayed to God to send them a little baby, but their prayers had not been answered.

Now the time came when it was the turn of Zacharias to go to Jerusalem to take his part, with other ministers, in the Temple service. Two men went in with Zacharias, one carrying a golden bowl full of incense, and the other a golden bowl full of burning coals. These they put on the altar and went out, leaving Zacharias alone. Zacharias was to take the incense and sprinkle it on the burning coals so as to make a thick fragrant smoke. "And the smoke of the incense, with the prayers of the saints, ascended up before God."

Then it was that the strange thing happened; for as this white-haired old man cast the incense on the coals and the place was filled with smoke, suddenly he saw an angel of the Lord standing beside him. And when Zacharias saw him, he was troubled, and fear fell upon him. But the angel said, "Fear not, Zacharias, for thy prayer is heard; and thy wife Elisabeth shall bear thee a son, and thou shalt call his name John. And thou shalt have joy and gladness; and many shall rejoice at his birth. And he shall go before the Lord." That is, the child, thus to be born, should be the herald of the King.

"I am an old man," [Zacharias] said, "and my wife well stricken in years." But the angel answered, "You do not know who I am. My name is Gabriel. I come to you straight from God. He has sent me to tell you these glad tidings. And now because you do not believe, you shall be dumb and not able to speak until this comes to pass." So he vanished out of sight.

Meanwhile, the people in great silence waiting without were wondering why Zacharias stayed so long in the Holy Place. And when he came out, and held up his hands in blessing but was speechless, and could only make signs to them, touching his lips and pointing to the sky, they knew that he had seen a vision.

And by and by, that which the angel had promised was fulfilled. The little boy came into the quiet house of Zacharias and Elisabeth. And when he was eight days old, according to the custom, he must be named. All their neighbors and cousins were glad that God had heard their prayer, and on that day they came together to rejoice with the happy father and mother. And they said, "Of course, the baby will be named Zacharias, after the name of his father."

"Not so," said Elisabeth, "but he shall be called John." And they asked Zacharias, making signs to him, for he seems to have been deaf as well as dumb. And he took a slate and wrote as they crowded about to see; and the sentence was, "His name is John." And at that moment his speech came back, and his mouth opened immediately, and his tongue was loosed, and he spake and praised God. And all who were in the house were filled with fear and wonder, and when they came out they spoke to everybody whom they met, saying, "Have you heard what has happened in the house of Zacharias? What manner of child shall this be?" But Zacharias and Elisabeth knew what he should be. They knew that the child John should be the prophet of the Highest, the herald of the King.

THE PRECURSOR

"As John of old before His face
   did go
To make the rough ways smooth,
   that all might know
The level road that leads to
   Bethlehem, lo,
I come," proclaims the snow.

—JOHN BANISTER TABB

GOD SENDS AN ANGEL

JIM BISHOP

Gabriel stood before her and saw a dark, modest child of fourteen. "Rejoice, child of grace," he said. "The Lord is your helper. You are blessed beyond all women." Mary did not like the sound of the last sentence. Her hands began to shake. Why should she, a little country girl, be blessed beyond all women? Did it mean that she was about to die? Was she being taken, perhaps, to a far-off place, never again to see her mother and her father and—and—Joseph?

She said nothing. She tried to look away, not only because of terror but because it was considered bad manners in Judea for one to stare directly into the eyes of another; but her eyes were magnetized. She stared, and lowered her eyes, and stared again.

Gabriel's voice softened. "Do not tremble, Mary," he said. "You have found favor in the eyes of God. Behold: you are to be a mother and to bear a son, and to call Him Jesus. He will be great: 'Son of the Most High' will be His title, and the Lord God will give to Him the throne of His father, David. He will be king over the house of Jacob forever, and to His kingship there will be no end.

"The Holy Spirit will come upon you, and the power of the Most High will overshadow you. For this reason the child to be born will be acclaimed 'Holy' and 'Son of God.'" She now understood the words, but they added to her bewilderment. What the angel was saying, she reasoned, was something for which the Jews had been waiting for centuries: a Messiah, a Saviour, God come to earth as He had promised long ago. Mary shook her head.

Not to her. Not to her.

Gabriel sensed that the child needed more proof. "Note,

moreover," he said, "your relative Elisabeth, in her old age, has also conceived a son and is now in her sixth month—she who was called 'barren.' Nothing indeed is impossible for God."

Her eyes lowered to the earthen floor, and her head inclined too. She comprehended. She also understood that the angel had told her about her old cousin Elisabeth, whom she had not seen in some time, so that the fruitfulness of her kinswoman would be the earthly seal of proof to the heavenly words. She was to be blessed by the Holy Spirit, and she would bear a male child who would be God. It was an enormous honor, but she had been taught to accept and obey the will of God from the first moments of early understanding.

"Regard me as the humble servant of the Lord," she murmured. "May all that you have said be fulfilled in me."

THE ANNUNCIATION

God whispered, and a silence fell;
   the world
Poised one expectant moment,
   like a soul
Who sees at heaven's threshold
   the unfurled
White wings of cherubim,
   the sea impearled,
And pauses, dazed, to comprehend
   the whole;
Only across all space God's
   whisper came
And burned about her heart
   like some white flame.

Then suddenly a bird's note
   thrilled the peace,
And earth again jarred noisily to life
With a great murmur as of many seas.
But Mary sat with hands clasped
   on her knees
And lifted eyes with all
   amazement rife,
And in her heart the rapture
   of the spring
Upon its first sweet day of blossoming.

—THEODOSIA GARRISON

These statues of the Annunciation are located in old Nazareth, where the Angel Gabriel is said to have appeared to Mary to tell her that she had been chosen to be the mother of Jesus. (Jeanne Conte)

II

IN BETHLEHEM

And the Word was made

flesh, and dwelt among us, (and

we beheld His glory, the glory as

of the only begotten of the

Father,) full of grace and truth.

–JOHN 1:14

THE LONG JOURNEY

FULTON OURSLER

And Joseph also went up from Galilee, out of the city of Nazareth, into Judaea, unto the city of David, which is called Bethlehem; (because he was of the house and lineage of David:) To be taxed with Mary his espoused wife, being great with child.

And so it was, that, while they were there, the days were accomplished that she should be delivered. And she brought forth her firstborn son, and wrapped Him in swaddling clothes, and laid Him in a manger; because there was no room for them in the inn.

—LUKE 2:4–7

(photo, pages 14–15)
Bethlehem, which means "house of bread," is located about five miles south of Jerusalem. It was both the ancestral home of David and the birthplace of Jesus.
(Erich Lessing/Art Resource)

From Nazareth it is a distance of seventy-five miles to Bethlehem of Judea. For Joseph and Mary and Anna and Joachim—the aged father and mother also had to go down to be counted—that made a three-day journey. The two women rode on stubborn little Galilean donkeys, while their men trudged alongside and held on to the reins.

Wayfarers by the thousands cluttered the highway, all leaving their homes because the Emperor of Rome had said that they must.

During the heat of the day they sang lustily from the psaltery: the brave and happy songs of David; several men had brought along little harps and plucked at the strings as they marched. So it was not a lonely journey and Mary did not suffer. Her light blue mantle was tucked back like a high collar rising behind her head, and the wind played with her hair; she was pale, and her face was much thinner; but her eyes were quiet and she remained very still. Not once did she join in the singing; she seemed to be listening and waiting.

"Mary, beloved, we are coming near to Shiloh."

"Is Shiloh a big place, Joseph?"

"Not so very big. Except in history. The teacher in the synagogue says it was there that the mother of Samuel came to pray for the gift of a child."

"Ah, she certainly had an answer to her prayers. We must keep on praying like that, Joseph."

Hearts were lighter the third morning because they expected to reach their journey's end before nightfall. Joseph was apprehensively watching his wife all day; he had been wakeful during the night and heard her sighing in dreams, and he kept praying that they would get safely to Bethlehem.

"Bethlehem!"

A shout went up. Throngs of the pilgrims began to sing the psalms of David again; and others, tired as they were, danced with joy in the dust.

The pair rested on the road for a few minutes as they gazed upon the serene landscape, the tall spurs of the hills, the wheat fields, the olive clumps, the fig trees—and many other trees: tall, strong in their green reach against blue sky and puffy white clouds.

"Those trees are wonderful, are they not?" asked Mary. It was her way of being casual in these last desperate hours. She knew he had a carpenter's eyes for such things, and he easily named for her the poplars and live oaks, the pines, the firs, and the tamarisks.

And as they renewed their steep climb into the town, Joseph kept determinedly talking. He had noticed a tightening of his wife's hands, a whitening of knuckles.

"The child must be coming," he told himself. "I will get her to a bed as quickly as possible. Meanwhile I will try to keep her mind busy with other things."

Now they entered the streets of Bethlehem, and the press of pilgrims was so great that the pair could scarcely move forward; no one would even listen to Joseph when he asked the way to a hotel; one urchin laughed in his face at such a question. Five hostelries they tried, but all were filled up. Joseph kept on doggedly; he forced his way through the door of the last tavern and demanded to talk to the host.

"My wife is ill," pleaded Joseph. "Her baby is about to be born."

The innkeeper was a stout and grumpy man with an enormous stomach. With red hands clasped in front of him, he gaped at these four Nazarenes, and it seemed to Joseph as if all mercy fled from his little eyes. Then, he curled fat fingers around his mouth and bawled hoarsely:

GATES AND DOORS

There was a gentle hostler
   (And blessed be his name!)
He opened up the stable
   The night Our Lady came.
Our Lady and Saint Joseph,
   He gave them food and bed,
And Jesus Christ has given him
   A glory round his head.

—JOYCE KILMER

17

"Sarah!"

His wife, just as stout as he was—she might have been himself in women's clothes—came shuffling from the back of the house.

"What do you want?" she demanded, hoarse voice a replica of his own.

"Look at this woman."

"I see her, yes."

"Please," implored Joseph, "for the love of God—"

"Don't you realize," growled Sarah, "the place is full? All Bethlehem is full. There's not a bed in the town tonight. But she can't have a baby here on the floor. We've got to do something. Gabriel!"

"There is one warm and comfortable place where we haven't put anybody yet."

"Is there now? Where? Just where?" demanded Gabriel.

"In the stable!"

"The stable!" echoed Joseph miserably, and Anna put her arms around Mary. But the young wife looked gratefully at the innkeeper's wife.

The Church of the Nativity in Bethlehem was built over the cave area that served as the stable in which it is believed Jesus was born. (Jean Higgins/Unicorn)

The stable was in a roomy cave that extended under the whole building of the inn. Joseph held Mary's hand as he led her down twisting stone steps to an earthen floor.

"Where are we going to put her down?" cried Anna distractedly.

Heaving and puffing, the stout Sarah came clumping down the stairs behind them, and after her Gabriel, puffing even louder than his wife, both clasping fresh bundles of straw. They laid a bed against the inner wall, which was warmer and not so damp, and they brought linen and a coverlet and a pillow for Mary's head.

Then Gabriel and Sarah had to leave them, for business was brisk upstairs, but both of them paused to give a hoarse, "God be with you tonight!" As their footsteps died away, the four at last felt relieved, if only to be alone. Anna helped Mary to undress, and then she went upstairs in search of jars of heated water, while Joseph stood near brooding.

"Why do we have no sign now?" he was asking himself. "Where is the angel? Why doesn't Anna hurry back?"

Anna soon came back with the water. She briskly exiled Joseph and Joachim through a rear door in the stable, bidding them to stay out until they were sent for. It was dark outside, the night air moist and cold.

And Joseph was trudging up and down in the dark area behind the stable. He fingered the pouch that held his store of coins and wondered whether he had enough money to see them through. The hours dragged on. Joachim had sat down on his haunches and soon fell asleep. But Joseph walked on like a man in a nightmare, waiting, praying, until at last and suddenly he heard the sound—a child's first cry.

In the dimmish light he knelt beside the bed of straw where Mary lay pale and weak but wide-eyed and with a small, brave smile for him.

"See!" she murmured.

Joseph was on his knees. Mary held out firm hands, lifting up her son, wrapped in Grandmother Anna's swaddling clothes—lifting Him up adoringly, the fate of the world reposing in the chalice of her hands.

Even in the first instant of seeing the child, Joseph was aware of something extraordinarily different about Him. Somehow he knew that this newborn baby, whose face was not red and crinkled but smooth and white, and whose expression was of such potent innocence and affection, had come into the world to get nothing and to give everything.

Mary of Bethlehem

When Mary came to Bethlehem,
To Bethlehem, to Bethlehem,
When Mary came to Bethlehem
And tarried near the Inn,
Every child in Bethlehem,
and every beast in Bethlehem
and every bird in Bethlehem,
Longed to be her kin.

When Mary rode from Bethlehem,
Everything was still—
All the birds of Bethlehem
sang Aves from the hill;
Little children ceased their play,
Lowly oxen turned her way,
Because she had been one of them
And greatly loved in Bethlehem.

—Mary King

TIDINGS OF GREAT JOY

ERMA FERRARI

And there were in the same country shepherds abiding in the field, keeping watch over their flock by night. And, lo, the angel of the Lord came upon them, and the glory of the Lord shone round about them: and they were sore afraid.

And the angel said unto them, Fear not: for, behold, I bring you good tidings of great joy, which shall be to all people.

And it came to pass, as the angels were gone away from them into heaven, the shepherds said one to another, Let us now go even unto Bethlehem, and see this thing which is come to pass, which the Lord hath made known unto us. And they came with haste, and found Mary, and Joseph, and the babe lying in a manger. And when they had seen it, they made known abroad the saying which was told them concerning this child.

–LUKE 2:8–10, 15–17

The midnight watch was nearly over before Bethlehem grew quiet. But at last all the visitors had found lodgings or had pitched their tents outside the city walls.

Not all the people of Bethlehem were asleep. Up in the hills, a group of shepherds were guarding their flocks from the dangers of the night. Now and then they sang softly to the sound of a flute.

"The stars are very bright tonight," young Nathan, the flute player, said. "And how close they seem."

His father nodded sleepily.

"Father! Father! Look!"

A dazzling light had enveloped the hillside. Terrified, the shepherds fell to their knees as an angel appeared within the light.

"Fear not," the angel said. "For, behold, I bring you good tidings of great joy, which shall be to all people. For unto you is born this day, in the city of David, a Saviour, which is Christ the Lord."

What words were these? Could it be true that the long-awaited Messiah had come? Wonderingly, the shepherds listened as the angel spoke again. "Ye shall find the babe wrapped in swaddling clothes, lying in a manger."

And suddenly the hillside rang with the song of a host of angels, praising God and saying, "Glory to God in the Highest."

So, leaving the precious flocks, the shepherds went down the hillside, rods and staffs in hand. Past the visitors' tents outside the wall and through the gates into the dark, silent town they went, looking for a newborn child. And finally, in a stable-cave cut neatly out of a rocky slope, they knew their

search was ended. No ordinary mother was this bending over the stone manger. Quietly, hesitatingly, the shepherds approached. Could this sleeping infant be the Messiah, the chosen deliverer of Israel? With awe, they bent over the manger. Joseph sat at one side, patiently quiet.

"The babe's name is Jesus," the young mother said.

Even unlearned shepherds knew the meaning of that name—God saves. Reverently, they knelt before their King. ⊛

These fields are about two miles east of Bethlehem, near the place where it is believed that the angels appeared to the shepherds on the night of Christ's birth. (Jeanne Conte)

THE SHEPHERD SPEAKS

Out of the midnight sky a great dawn broke,
And a voice singing flooded us with song.
In David's city was He born, it sang.
A Saviour, Christ the Lord. Then while I sat
Shivering with the thrill of that great cry,
A mighty choir a thousandfold more sweet
Suddenly sang, Glory to God, and Peace,

Peace on the earth; my heart, almost unnerved
By that swift loveliness, would hardly beat.
Speechless we waited till the accustomed night
Gave us no promise more of sweet surprise;
Then scrambling to our feet, without a word
We started through the fields to find the Child.

—JOHN ERSKINE

THE FIRST SHADOW FALLS

ALICE M. DARTON

Simeon was an old man going down to his grave at the end of a life of righteousness. Ardently had he prayed for the consolation of Israel, so sorely beset and so sadly in need of redemption. And his faith had been rewarded: the Holy Spirit had revealed that he should not see death before he had seen the Christ.

How this was to be fulfilled, Simeon did not know. Probably like most Jews, he expected to see an angelic sort of being with unlimited earthly power at his command—a kind of superman. Simeon, however, had no arrogance of spirit. When he entered the Temple, led by the Spirit, and perceived that the child of this poor, inconspicuous mother was the expected Messiah, he accepted this fact with perfect submission of his will and blessed God.

Again Mary and Joseph found that God had disclosed His mercy, and in the same unexpected way as to the shepherds. Had the priest who had redeemed their child uttered the words of Simeon, they would not have been surprised; he stood to them as the churchly authority, as the chosen of God. But he had held this Holy Child in his arms, entirely unconscious of His identity; he had received the redemption sum and recited the benedictions in a purely perfunctory manner. They had turned from him, believing that God intended to conceal the identity of Jesus even in His Temple. But Simeon—not a priest, not a Levite, but simply a just and devout man—accosted them.

Simeon's heart yearned over this little family, and as he restored the child again to His mother's arms he blessed Mary and Joseph, upon whom rested the responsibility of this glorious child. And God permitted him to see some of

the future, and he spoke to Mary the first words of warning: "Behold, this child is set for the fall and for the resurrection of many in Israel, and for a sign which shall be contradicted. And thy own soul a sword shall pierce, that, out of many hearts, thoughts may be revealed."

This was the first shadow that fell upon Mary and the babe. Their future together, even though unknown, had seemed to stretch radiantly before her. This radiance was now dimmed. What sword could pierce her soul but sorrow for Him? This child, for whom she would lay down her life, whom as "handmaiden" she would serve forever, was to meet opposition and suffering. That message of Simeon was the shock which took away the last traces of girlishness from the young mother, implanting in her in its stead that serious and understanding conformity to the will of God which was to increase with the years and hold her steadfast at the foot of the cross.

In spite of the strife present in Bethlehem today, it continues to be a place of celebration, visited by many thousands each year. (Jeanne Conte)

THE WISE MEN

DALLAS LORE SHARP

*Now when Jesus was born in
Bethlehem of Judaea in the days
of Herod the king, behold, there
came wise men from the east to
Jerusalem. And being warned of
God in a dream that they should
not return to Herod, they
departed into their own country
another way.*

–MATTHEW 2:1, 12

Melchior, Caspar, and Balthasar may have been the names of the Wise Men from the East. We do not know. We do not even know that there were three of them. All that we are sure of is the meager story that Saint Matthew tells us. Tradition has named them and given us their history.

It was shortly after the presentation in the Temple that these Wise Men, or Magi, appeared in Jerusalem asking for the Messiah—King of Israel, whose star they had seen at its rising, and to whom they now came to pay homage.

These Magi were not of the evil class so often spoken of as sorcerers and practicers of magic but were wise men in truth, priests—sages from the East who were deeply learned in the sciences, especially astrology.

It is probable that they came from Persia. For two centuries Judaea was a province of the Persian Empire, and many of the Jews never returned to Palestine after the exile but remained in scattered communities over the lands of the East, where their descendants were still living. Then the Jewish and Persian faiths had much in common, and the interests between the two countries at this time were close and mutual. The East was almost as full of Jews as the West. Judaism went with the Jew—a Jew was nothing if not religious—and Jewish ideas, especially the burning belief that a great prince, the Messiah, was about to be born in Palestine, were diffused through every land.

The Persians were well acquainted with the prophecies concerning Him, both those current among the Jews, and that of their own prophet, Balaam; and they also knew that the expected time was close at hand.

It was this new "star" in the heaven that confirmed

their faith. It announced to them His birth and started them on their journey of homage.

The Wise Men came directly to Jerusalem and to Herod, as the one most likely to tell them where the new King might be found.

Their appearance was quickly noised about Jerusalem, and it roused excitement, not only in the palace of Herod, but over all the city.

It was a time of expectation and unrest. The yoke of foreign tyranny galled the people; clouds of the coming storm rolled dark across the horizon; prayers, like the mutterings of distant thunder, rose continually for the Messiah; literature was completely Messianic; messiahs rose everywhere; and Israel only awaited the word of the true King. When, therefore, news spread among the rabbis that Magi from Persia, from the land of the prophet Balaam—a prophet of the Messiah, whom the Jews thoroughly honored—had seen the star of the new King, their excitement led them almost into open rebellion.

But Herod was still the master in Jerusalem. The Wise Men had gone to him with the question, "Where is the King of the Jews born?"

COVENTRY CAROL

Lullay, Thou little tiny Child,
By, by lully, lullay.
Lullay, Thou little tiny Child,
By, by lully, lullay.

O sisters too, how may we do,
For to preserve this day.
This poor youngling for whom
we sing
By, by lully, lullay.

Herod the king, in his raging,
Charge he hath this day,
His men of might, in his own
sight,
All young children to slay.

That woe is me, poor Child for
Thee!
And ever morn and day,
For Thy parting neither say nor
sing,
By, by lully, lullay.

–AUTHOR UNKNOWN

Little did they know Herod. He would have been glad to answer their question! The news struck terror to his heart. He immediately called together his high priests and all the rabbis, and with his usual cunning, asked of them where the King was to be born, having previously found out from the Magi the exact time they first saw the star arise.

With one voice the priests and teachers told Herod that the Messiah should be born in Bethlehem. This was all he wanted to know, and now, with pretended interest in His welfare, Herod secretly sent the Wise Men on to Bethlehem with his friendly and imperial wish that when they had found the Child they quickly return, that he also might go and pay homage.

As they left Jerusalem, to their joy the star arose before them and stood in the heavens over Bethlehem. Passing through the low gate of the town, they found the Holy Family—now living in a "house"—and spread their gifts before the Child.

The Wise Men had found the infant Messiah; but as they were about to leave for Jerusalem to deliver to Herod the anxiously awaited news, they were warned in a dream of the real purpose of Herod and they hastened from Bethlehem to "depart into their own country another way."

In his malignant cunning Herod had graciously inquired of them what time the star first appeared. They told him that it first rose about two years previous to their visit. That was fact number one. He then made the scribes tell him where the child should be born. They had said Bethlehem was the place. This was fact number two. What more did he want? He knew the time and the place, and now the Wise Men might return to him or they might not. If they came, then only one child would be murdered; if they did not come, why, he had as many assassins as there were children in Bethlehem, and what were the lives of

twenty or thirty babes, if in any way they threatened him?

The Wise Men told Joseph of their warning dream. Joseph was prepared also by the message that came to him in his sleep. Startled by the dream, he rose, made ready their few belongings, saddled them upon the ass behind Mary and the Child, and passed through the gates of the silent town, out under the midnight skies, a fugitive, guided only by mysterious Providence.

Egypt was their destination, and passing through Hebron and Beersheba, they were far into the desert when Herod's soldiers entered Bethlehem with orders to slay every male child of two years old or under.

Excavations along the outside walls of Old Jerusalem show intriguing detail of what the city might have looked like during the time of Jesus. (Jeanne Conte)

27

FLIGHT INTO EGYPT

H. W. VAN DER VAART SMIT

And when they were departed, behold, the angel of the Lord appeareth to Joseph in a dream, saying, Arise, and take the young child and His mother, and flee into Egypt, and be thou there until I bring thee word: for Herod will seek the young child to destroy Him.

When he arose, he took the young child and His mother by night, and departed into Egypt: And was there until the death of Herod: that it might be fulfilled which was spoken of the Lord by the prophet, saying, Out of Egypt have I called My Son.

Then Herod, when he saw that he was mocked of the Wise Men, was exceeding wroth, and sent forth, and slew all the children that were in Bethlehem, and in all the coasts thereof, from two years old and under, according to the time which he had diligently inquired of the Wise Men.

—MATTHEW 2:13–16

It is quite clear why Joseph arose in the night and fled with mother and child. He did not hesitate one minute after the decision was made. "Arise," said the angel; it was then night, and he dared not wait till daybreak. His obedience to the word of the angel was all the more prompt now that he knew he could at last escape the dangers that haunted him day and night. Had it not been for his firm resolve earlier to wait out the time until he could visit the Temple with Mary and the child, he would have left Bethlehem long before this. Learning now of the immediate danger, he did not hesitate to leave.

The journey through the desert to Egypt lasted somewhat longer than a week, and of course for the mother and child a mule was necessary on the journey. That such an animal was available in the middle of the night leads us to suppose that he had kept it with him since his departure from Nazareth, so that it was now of use to him again. In itself the journey was not without danger, for the bands of Judas of Galilee made the desert between Israel and Egypt unsafe for travel. But refugees from Herod's kingdom would not receive bad treatment at their hands.

We do not know if Herod struck right away, but it is a safe guess that he did, for the angel urged haste in his warning to Joseph. The flight was probably just at the right time. Although the king may not have received word immediately that the Wise Men had departed for home without returning to him, he learned soon enough. Perhaps the king also heard how great was the enthusiasm of the many visitors to the Temple who heard Simeon's and Anna's words. All of this would have been more than enough to goad the irascible Herod to action. He dispatched his band of assassins.

He had already found out from the Wise Men how old the child might be. The planetary conjunction ran its course in three stages; the child could have been born even during the first stage, and three-fourths of a year had elapsed since then. In short, the king ordered all boys of two years old and under to be killed. He did not make the age bracket too narrow; it mattered little to him whether a few boys more or less were killed. "All male children of two years and under in Bethlehem and vicinity are to be killed," was the way his order read. And the order was carried out.

Soon Bethlehem saw itself surrounded, and the soldiers killed the infants as they were commanded. The number is differently reported; some say from thirteen to fifteen children, others say from twenty to thirty. We consider the latter number more probable; the locale was indeed small, but the "entire vicinity" would not have been reckoned as small by soldiers who well knew how the king wanted his commands to be carried out.

Thus the events of Christmas in Bethlehem come to an end with blood and tears; the joy over all the things the shepherds and the Magi experienced and told about ends in deep pain. And so the Messiah enters the shadow of the cross even as He comes into the world.

They knew in Bethlehem that at least the little boy Jesus did not fall victim to Herod's blood bath. Perhaps people even told the soldiers that He had escaped, just to save their own children. Yet orders were orders, especially with Herod, and the fact that the child they were seeking had escaped, as people had said, would have been carefully concealed by the soldiers to save their own necks, or possibly to avoid being sent out to search further in the dangerous deserts to the south. They rendered their report: What we were ordered to do has been done; no one can have escaped in Bethlehem and its surroundings. ✳

ALL THE ROAD TO EGYPT

All the road to Egypt
    Sang to see them pass,
The Child asleep on Mary's arm,
Old Joseph,
    shielding them from harm,
The Angel, beautiful as hope,
Leading by a twist of rope
    The little, gray-coat ass.

All the road to Egypt
    Knelt to see them pass,
The Child's dear head haloed gold,
Madonna's robe in many a fold
Of changing blue
    like shimmering wave,
Whose falling grace a glory gave
    Even to the dusty ass.

All the road to Egypt
    Danced to see them pass,
Old Joseph's cloak of cinnamon,
The Angel's restless wings that shone
Green as the trees of Paradise,
And like some curious, chased device
    A little silver ass.

All the road to Egypt
    Bloomed to feel them pass,
So raced the sap in stem and root
The withered fig tree sprang to fruit;
The palm and olive bowed their load
To Mary's lips; that purple road
    Bore thistles for the ass.

—KATHARINE LEE BATES

III

A CHILD GROWS IN NAZARETH

And He went down with them, and came to Nazareth, and was subject unto them: but His mother kept all these sayings in her heart. And Jesus increased in wisdom and stature, and in favour with God and man.

–LUKE 2:51–52

THE GOOD THAT GREW IN NAZARETH

EDNA MADISON BONSER

A fictionalized account of Jesus,
here called Joshua ben Joseph—son of Joseph—and his father.

Into the little carpenter's shop, with its saws and hammers and planes, came many kinds of people on many errands.

Caravans from far-off places passed through and sometimes stopped for water or food; travelers on foot or on donkey or camel often stopped; and often peddlers, storytellers, or teachers with their followers would stop overnight.

Sometimes a wheel was broken on the rocky road or a saddle needed mending. Then a carpenter was needed, and the owner of the wheel or saddle came to father Joseph's shop. The little boy Joshua had a fine chance to see and hear all that went on, for He could stand close to father Joseph and hand him a tool now and then.

Once a poor Jewish man came with a broken yoke complaining bitterly that he had been robbed and beaten by tax collectors who had overtaken him, and, declaring that their horses needed fodder, had taken all that he had and left him beaten and half dead by the roadside.

"They said," cried the man, wiping the blood and dust from his face with his arm, "that a dog of a Jew is fit to be kicked, and they struck me with my own ox-yoke rather than touch me with their hands."

"Did you not tell them," cried father Joseph, "that you had already paid your full tax to Caesar and that nothing more was due to the government from you for another year?"

"What cared they for what I could say or for what is just and right? God smite them," he cried, fiercely. "God curse—"

(photo, pages 30–31)
Jesus was born in Bethlehem in Judea;
after the family's flight into Egypt, they
returned to Nazareth in Galilee where
Jesus grew up. The rolling hillsides of
Judea were often terraced in ancient
times so the land could be better uti-
lized. (Jeanne Conte)

32

"Speak not of God's vengeance in this place," father Joseph said, sternly, glancing at the little Boy. "Run, lad, and tell your mother that one is here who needs her balsams and healing lotions and stay you with the little ones while she comes to this poor man's help. He has been cruelly treated and needs pity and care."

Joshua ran quickly, glad to escape to the sweet peace of the little house, from the sight of the angry, blood-stained man whom the arrogant Publicans had beaten and robbed. Later, when the man was sleeping, father Joseph told Him some things that helped Him to understand and filled His heart with a great longing and desire to help all men everywhere to be merciful and just.

"We—I mean the Jews—my Boy," father Joseph had said, "are ruled by the Romans. There was a time, hundreds of years ago, when we lived happily in this beautiful country and were ruled by our own kings. The country was ours. But we were too few and too weak, too quarrelsome and proud, too wicked and forgetful of God if the truth were told, to resist our enemies; and they swept down on us from the north in all the savagery of cruel warfare and carried away our people into slavery. That was but the beginning of our troubles. First came the Assyrians . . . then, as if God had altogether forgotten us, came the Persians. [They] destroyed our sacred city of Jerusalem and the Temple and drove before them into captivity all whom the Assyrians had left.

"It is a sorrowful story. Perhaps you would rather not know it," said father Joseph, seeing the little Boy's wide eyes fill with tears.

"No, no! Tell me all!" He cried. "They are my people. I must know how to understand."

"The Persians were kinder to us than the Assyrians had been," father Joseph went on. "True, we were slaves and they exacted labor and tribute from us, but after a long time some

FROM NAZARETH

Comes any good from Nazareth?
The scornful challenge as of old
Is flung on many a jeering breath
From cloistered cells and marts of gold.

Comes any good from Nazareth?
Behold, the mighty Nazarene,
The Lord of life, the Lord of death,
Through warring ages walks serene.

One touch upon His garment's fringe
Still heals the hurt of bitter years.
Before Him yet the demons cringe,
He gives the wine of joy for tears.

O city of the Carpenter,
Upon the hillslope old and gray,
The world amid its pain and stir
Turns yearning eyes on thee today.

For He who dwelt in Nazareth,
And wrought with toil of hand
    and brain,
Alone gives victory to faith
Until the day He comes again.

—MARGARET E. SANGSTER

From the time of the family's return from Egypt until He left to begin His ministry, Jesus spent most of His life in the town of Nazareth. He became so identified with the town that He became known as "Jesus of Nazareth." (Erich Lessing/Art Resource)

of our most loyal people were allowed to come back and begin to rebuild the Temple and the wall about Jerusalem. All might have gone well had not the Greeks conquered the Persians in battle more than three hundred years ago and so become our masters.

"The Greeks permitted us to live in our own land but exacted from us such tribute in money and labor that we were helpless. They tried by every means in their power to destroy our faith in God and compelled us to worship their gods. They even placed a statue of their god, Jupiter, before the most holy altar of the living God in our Temple and compelled men and women to bow down to it and worship it. In this terrible trouble God helped us, for He raised up a courageous Jew to defy the Greeks. This was Mattathias. He utterly refused to worship Jupiter and, together with his five brave sons, escaped to the hills and resisted the Greeks until freedom was won. Then once more, for a hundred years, Israel had her own kings who ruled our people with wisdom and justice."

There was silence in the little shop broken only by the tap, tap of hammer on wood. Then Joshua said, "But these were Roman tax collectors who beat and robbed the poor fellow yonder. How came they to be our masters?"

"Our little country, my Boy, is like the grain between the upper and the nether millstones, for we lie between the great countries which are always quarreling and fighting to see which shall rule the world: the Persians, the Greeks, or the Egyptians. But after a while a new race of fighting men challenged all of these powers. The Romans with their wealth, their skill, and their arrogant spirit came. They have an emperor whom they call Caesar. Now Caesar rules the world. And we, to whom God gave the land, pay tribute to him.

It seems that we are permitted to live," father Joseph went

on, bitterly, "that we may make money to pay taxes to the Romans, and that our young men may fill their armies with slaves and soldiers. We suffer always such treatment as this poor man has suffered, and we are powerless. We who were once so great and glorious! We who are God's chosen people!

"O God! Our God!" father Joseph prayed with the tears streaming down his cheeks, "send us a Saviour to lead us out of this bondage. Forsake us not but remember Thy people how they suffer. Fulfill Thy promises in us, Our Gracious Jehovah.

"Yes," he added in a calmer tone to the wide-eyed little Boy, "God has promised us a Messiah who will right our wrongs and help us to take our true place and power in the world. When He comes, all wrong shall be righted and we shall dwell in peace and happiness."

No more was said for a long time. The little Boy seemed to be thinking too deeply to ask any more questions. When evening came, the poor man wakened and seemed much happier. Mother had washed his wounds, bound them with clean strips of cloth, and given him food. He was almost cheerful. "It is good," he said, "almost worth being robbed and beaten, to find such kind and generous friends. I shall never forget, and sometime if I can serve you in return I shall do so."

"Leave the yoke," said father Joseph. "I will mend it and my work shall cost you nothing."

"The God of our fathers forfend and bless thee. The Lord bless thee and keep thee," said the man, earnestly.

That evening when they were sitting in the twilight upon the roof of their small home, Joshua crept close to His mother and whispered. "When I am a man I shall help the poor and the sick, as you do. But why does God let us suffer so? Why does He let us be hurt?"

"I know not, little Son, except that He wishes us to learn to be pitiful and tenderhearted."

THE BOY JESUS

Once, measuring His height,
    He stood
      Beneath a cypress tree,
And, leaning back against the wood,
      Stretched wide His arms for me;
Whereat a brooding mother-dove
Fled fluttering from her nest above.

At evening He loved to walk
Among the shadowy hills and talk
      Of Bethlehem;
But if perchance there passed us by
The paschal lambs, He'd look
      at them
In silence, long and tenderly;
And when again He'd try to speak,
I've seen the tears upon His cheek.

—JOHN BANISTER TABB

And the child grew, and waxed strong in spirit, filled with wisdom: and the grace of God was upon Him.

–LUKE 2:40

Is not this the carpenter, the son of Mary, the brother of James, and Joses, and of Juda, and Simon? and are not His sisters here with us?

–MARK 6:3

JESUS IN HIS FAMILY

WINIFRED KIRKLAND

This author conjectures on the family life of Jesus as a child.

We need to look clear-eyed at that Nazareth home, and at the ten-year-old Jesus in it, in order to realize, first and forever, that the home life of the child Jesus could not have been easy. It was a one-room house; in it there were at least seven children. Under the combined Roman and Jewish taxation, the family must have been cruelly poor.

The New Testament mentions Jesus' brothers in several different connections. Mark, writing as Peter's secretary, has been describing Jesus' abrupt emergence from obscurity into astounding popularity, a homekeeping carpenter suddenly able to heal, to teach, to preach, so that all the countryside stood amazed and awed. Then in contrast there came hurrying from Nazareth a little band of Jesus' relatives, unbelieving and alarmed. They came with ropes to bind Him as a lunatic and to take Him home, declaring, "He has gone raving mad!"

Later gospel references reveal the brothers of Jesus in the same light. The evangelist John reports a conversation full of taunts and ridicule. No brother rushes to Jesus' side when the Nazareth mob rises against Him. No brother is present at the cross. Yet afterward the "brethren of the Lord" are mentioned as members of the brave persecuted church at Jerusalem. The brother James became a leader among the early Christians. Obviously the brothers of Jesus during His lifetime had little sympathy for His work.

We may conjecture that from His earliest years Jesus had the same attitude toward His family that He later, without exception, showed in all His contacts with all men and women, the attitude of reverent discovery. His readiness to discover His brothers, as they grew beside Him, may perhaps have meant constant fresh discovery of Himself and of His capacities for patience and for adaptation.

Ever present, ever tender, as a background for that sprouting horde of children, stand Joseph and Mary. Mary's life was no easy one: poverty-stricken, heavily-worked, and often anxious, especially for that firstborn son. Household serenity must have been for her a difficult attainment, but surely she achieved high and holy peace, or so sensitive a child could never have grown to be so joyous a man. Mary lived in a period when women were frankly looked down upon. In sharp contrast with His contemporaries, how did Jesus regard women? It seems as if a little boy may once have watched a woman in a one-room peasant home, and, watching her, have learned His reverence for all women.

And Joseph's daily life at home is also to be found written upon the teachings of Jesus. In that crowded household Jesus watched a village carpenter, quiet, gentle, tender, humbly trying to guard and rear his brood. What the boy Jesus, watching, came to think about Joseph is to be guessed from what the word "father" came to mean in His teaching.

And together in a devout, high, united endeavor to fulfill God's will for man and wife, Joseph and Mary wrote upon Jesus' mind a conception of marriage so high that even today it sets His teaching apart from that of all others. The home a humble man and woman, true to the ideals of their race, achieved, became a fitting nursery for a child entrusted to them by God for their rearing. What Jesus, looking back, came to think of His own family life is best shown by the fact that He pictured even the kingdom of heaven as a home full of happy children, which no one might enter except as a little child.

THE HIDDEN YEARS

The hidden years at Nazareth!
   How deep and still they seem,
Like rivers flowing in the dark
   Or waters in a dream!
Like waters under Syrian stars
   Reflecting lights above,
Repeating in their silent depths
   The wonder of God's love!

The hidden years at Nazareth!
   How clear and true they lie,
As open to the smile of God
   As to the Syrian sky!
As open to the heart of man
   As to the genial sun,
With dreams of vast adventuring
   And deeds of kindness done!

The hidden years at Nazareth!
   How radiant they rise,
With life and death in balance laid
   Before a lad's clear eyes!
O Soul of Youth, forever choose,
   Forgetting fate or fear,
To live for truth or die with God,
   Who stands beside thee here!

—ALLEN EASTMAN CROSS

THE QUESTION
THE WISE MEN ASKED

EDNA MADISON BONSER

*A fictionalized account of Jesus, here called Joshua,
and His conversation with the Temple leaders at age twelve.*

Now His parents went to Jerusalem every year at the feast of the passover. And when He was twelve years old, they went up to Jerusalem after the custom of the feast.

And it came to pass, that after three days they found Him in the Temple, sitting in the midst of the doctors, both hearing them, and asking them questions. And all that heard Him were astonished at His understanding and answers. And when they saw Him, they were amazed: and His mother said unto Him, Son, why hast Thou thus dealt with us? behold, Thy father and I have sought Thee sorrowing.

And He said unto them, How is it that ye sought Me? wist ye not that I must be about My Father's business? And they understood not the saying which He spake unto them.

–LUKE 2:41–42, 46–50

On the Temple porch a little group of wise men sat and talked together. The Feast of Passover was finished, but crowds of people still lingered in Jerusalem. Some of them found it pleasant to visit with relatives and friends. Some had business to attend to, while a few wished to linger in the Temple and learn more of the wisdom of the Rabbis. Among these was the little boy, Joshua.

From the time He had knelt with father Joseph and joined in the prayers and the chants, watched the sacrifices, and heard the readings of the law and the prophets, He had lost all thought or sense of other things. Whole groups of people were leaving Jerusalem. By every gate they were going out towards their homes. But of these He thought not at all. Each morning He went swiftly back to the Temple and stayed there as long as He could.

Even mother was forgotten and father Joseph. If He thought at all of them, it was only to tell Himself, "They will understand that I must be here. They will look for Me here." Then He was lost again in thoughts of God.

There was a question He wanted to ask the scholars and teachers in the Temple, a question that had lain unanswered in His mind since Ruth's going away. He had asked it of Rabbi ben Ezra without getting an answer that satisfied Him. "Perhaps," He thought, "the old man does not know the answer." He had asked mother and father Joseph, but they had not told Him what He wished to know. Now He was determined to ask the wise teachers of the Temple. They surely could tell Him.

When He saw them, sitting together on the porch in order that they might talk freely with the people, He went and waited silently until one spoke to Him. He seemed very small and lonely there in His white tunic, His bright hair falling over His shoulders, His eyes glowing with eagerness, His face lighted from the glow of a deep inner peace into a rare beauty.

"Is there a question you would like to ask, my son?"

"I wanted to ask," began the little boy, then hesitated. "Rabbi ben Ezra said it was a deep question. Perhaps that means it cannot be answered, but it means so much to me. Ruth was good," He hurried on. "But she died. Her mother and Dinah and I had done no wrong. Yet we miss her so. Our hearts ache. Why—why?" He paused. "I can't say it as I should, but perhaps you understand. You are so wise," He finished.

All of the learned men were listening. Now they looked at each other in amazement.

"Where is your home, lad?" one asked Him.

"In Nazareth of Galilee, good master."

"Are you a Son of the Commandments?"

"I am but twelve, good master. In another year I shall be old enough to understand. But speak before Me now. It may be I can remember until I am older. Your words of wisdom will be in My mind. Even now I understand more than you might think."

The Western Wall, commonly called the Wailing Wall, is a remnant of the second Temple of Jerusalem. It is a destination for visitors from all over the world. (Zefa/H. Armstrong Roberts)

AT NAZARETH

A little Child, a Joy-of-heart,
    with eyes
Unsearchable, He grew in Nazareth,
His daily speech so innocently wise
That all the town went telling:
    "Jesus saith."

    –KATHARINE LEE BATES

39

JESUS IN THE TEMPLE

With His kind mother, who partakes
*   thy woe,*
Joseph, turn back; see where your
    Child doth sit,
Blowing, yea blowing out those
    sparks of wit
Which Himself on the doctors
    did bestow.
The Word but lately could
    not speak, and lo,
It suddenly speaks wonders;
    whence comes it,
That all which was, and all which
    should be writ,
A shallow-seeming child should
    deeply know?
His Godhead was not soul to
    His manhood,
Nor had time mellowed Him to this
    ripeness;
But as for one which hath
    a long task, 'tis good,
With the sun to begin His business,
He in His age's morning
    thus began,
By miracles exceeding power of man.

—JOHN DONNE

"The lad asks the age-old question of why, if our God is just as we believe Him to be, He still allows those who love and serve Him to suffer," broke in a deep voice, harsh and cold. "He is a lad wise beyond his years. Answer him, good masters. My ears await your wisdom. Yet speak cautiously. He who confounds man's wisdom sometimes speaks through the lips of babes."

But one of the teachers, a man with a long white beard and kindly smiling lips, drew the little boy into the circle of his arms and said, "It is clear to us that you have indeed thought beyond your years that this deep question should trouble you. It has troubled many and is not yet answered.

"But there is an old, old story that helps some too. It is about a man called Job. He was a good man, wise and rich and happy. He had great flocks and herds, many children, a beautiful home, and all that makes life happy and worthwhile. He had faith in God. He did no evil."

"Now God knew and loved Job and was proud of him. And one day He said to Satan, 'Did you see My servant, Job, how good he is and how he loves Me?'

"'Yes,' answered Satan. 'No wonder Job is good. You have given him everything a man could desire. But take away all his wealth, his good reputation, his children, and his home, and see what Job will do. He will turn against You and hate You.'

"'I do not think he will,' God answered. 'I have such confidence in Job that I will let you do all these things to him just to prove to you that he is good. I believe he will still trust in Me and serve Me. Go and do what you will. Job will be true to Me.'

"So Satan went away. First he caused all of Job's flocks and herds to be destroyed so that he was left poor.

"Job mourned and wept, but he was true to God.

"Then Satan caused all of Job's children to be killed.

"Job mourned and wept more than before, but he was

true to God. Then Satan caused a great sickness to come to Job. He was covered with boils from his head to his feet. Poor and childless and sick with a loathsome disease, Job sat in the ashes and mourned, but he did not forsake God.

"Even his wife said to him, 'Why don't you curse God and die?'

"But Job said, 'God sends us good. Why should He not send evil? I will still believe in God.' And because he still believed in God's justice, he said, 'What if all this does happen now? I know that even after I am dead I shall behold God.'

"When you are older, lad, you may read the whole story for yourself. It is enough now for you to know that Job was the first man to believe that even death could not end all. That a just God will balance things up, even if He has to provide another life after death in which to do it. Like Job, my lad, we do not clearly understand; but, like him, we have faith that God's justice will satisfy us here or in the hereafter."

Seeing the boy's face uplifted and shining, the wise old teacher said, "What think you, lad? Shall this come to pass?"

"I see more clearly now," said the boy. "Not even death can take the good people away from God, for He is Good."

There was a stirring about the door. Someone had come in and was calling. The little boy looked toward the doorway. Mother stood there holding out her arms.

"Son, son," she called. "We have looked for You in sorrow. We have been so worried and frightened. Why have You treated us so?"

"I thought that you would know that I would be here. You would surely know that I must begin to do God's work in the world."

"Yes, I do know," Mother answered. "But come home with us now. When You are older you shall do what You will."

"I will come," said the little boy gently. ❂

CHILD

The young child, Christ, is straight
    and wise
And asks questions of the old men:
    questions
Found under running water for all
    children,
And found under shadows thrown
    on still waters
By tall trees looking downwards,
    old and gnarled,
Found to the eyes of children alone,
    untold,
Singing a low song in the loneliness.
And the young child, Christ,
    goes asking,
And the old men answer nothing
    and only know love
For the young child, Christ,
    straight and wise.

—CARL SANDBURG

LEAVING
HIS NAZARETH HOME

EDWIN McNEILL POTEAT

We can only guess at how Jesus left home to begin His ministry. In this account, Jesus announces to His mother that He must go to do His Father's work.

IN GALILEE

Erect in youthful grace and radiant
    With spirit forces, all
        imparadised
In a divine compassion, down
    the slant
    Of these remembering hills He
    came, the Christ.

Should not the glowing lilies of the
    field
    With keener splendor mark His
    footprints yet?
Prints of the gentle feet whose
    passing healed
    All blight from Tabor unto
    Olivet?

–KATHARINE LEE BATES

The soft, bright edge of day had hardly pushed over the eastern ridge when the gate to the house of Joseph opened quietly and a tall figure bent slightly as He entered. His step was elastic and His countenance was as bright as if for the moment He had captured all the radiance of the dawn in His face. Nothing about His manner bespoke an all-night vigil on the mountaintop. He crossed the yard and listened at the door. No one seemed yet to be astir. He went into the shop. On a shelf was a toy He had whittled on in odd hours, a tiny yoke of oxen hitched to a plow. He blew the dust off it and put it on the bench as He brushed aside the debris of the previous day's work with His foot. He looked lovingly about the shop—at its dusty walls and shelves and the little piles of sawdust that He loved to run through His stout fingers. Then He picked up the toy and recrossed the yard to His mother's door. She called His name softly, and He entered her room and seated Himself beside her on the bed. She stroked His face fondly and noted the tiny wooden oxen in His hand.

"My time has come," He said suddenly. She clutched tightly at her heart and then breathed deeply as if in resignation to a destiny she had long known she could not escape.

"My time is come," He said again, His eyes lighted with an unearthly fire. "My Father is moving the hearts of the sons of men. Down in the valley John gathers to him those who need repair, whose hearts are broken with folly, whose bodies are broken with sin. They come from Jerusalem and from Judea to be baptized, confessing their sins."

He paused, and Mary leaned toward Him. A look of desperate inquiry burned in her eyes. He stood up and gripped her shoulders at arm's length with His powerful hands and then held her fiercely against Him long and breathlessly. It was the moment of farewell she had dreamed of and dreaded, but no word was given her to speak.

At length He said, picking up the little toy again, "I shall stop for a fig and curd at

This roadway between Jerusalem and Tel Aviv likely supports the same type of plant life Jesus may have encountered on His travels. (Jeff Greenberg/Unicorn)

Dimnah. The babes will like this; for several days I have been making it for them." He smiled reflectively, and for a moment the austere mood seemed to drop from Him. And then with a tenderness His mother was never to forget, He put His arm about her and led her to the door. He raised His hand and pointed down the valley. It was gold and blue in the early light. They walked slowly through the gate and stopped. Once again He pointed down the valley, but neither spoke. Her eyes were bright with tears as He kissed her forehead. Then down the alleyway He strode with strong, confident steps; and as He turned the corner that would lose Him from her sight, she raised her hand weakly. He returned her salute boldly and then was gone, never again to be known as the Son of Mary, but henceforth to be called the Son of Man.

JESUS IS BAPTIZED

JEAN STEINMANN

A VOICE FROM HEAVEN

Now had the great Proclaimer,
    with a voice cried
Repentance, and heaven's kingdom
    nigh at hand
To all baptized: to His great
    baptism flocked
With awe the regions round,
    and with them came
From Nazareth the son of Joseph,
    deemed unmarked, unknown;
but Him the Baptist soon descried,
    divinely warned, and witness
        bore
As to His worthier,
    nor was long
His witness unconfirmed: on
    Him baptized
Heaven opened, and in likeness
    of a dove
The Spirit descended, while the
    Father's voice
From Heaven pronounced Him
    His belovèd Son.

–JOHN MILTON

Jesus was about thirty when He joined John's desert entourage. Like many of His compatriots, He was of royal descent—that is, a little of David's blood ran in His veins. But His circumstances were comparatively humble. He was from the village of Nazareth, a carpenter and cartwright who spoke Aramaic with a northern accent and whose early education must have been restricted to the village school and the local synagogue. He knew Hebrew and probably understood Greek too.

His Galilean origin also equipped Him with traits characteristic of the better sort of northern provincial: hardheaded realism, broad-mindedness, the common touch, a certain prickly defiance when dealing with scornfully superior Judeans.

The religion which both He and His family followed was Orthodox Temple Judaism, modified in one or two respects by old-fashioned habits such as adherence to the old traditional calendar and a marked weakness for certain practices of the Essenes—ascetic self-denial, baptism, sharing property in common, communal meals of bread and wine, a contempt for money. On the other hand, He displayed little or no regard for the monastic ideal, with its strict discipline, blind obedience, and quasi-military organization.

Jesus had been brought up in a tradition of ideas very much akin to those held by good Pharisees. He believed firmly in the resurrection of the dead and intercession by angels in human affairs; yet there was much that He found to dislike about these strict sectarians: their ostentatious habits, their self-righteousness, their holier-than-thou attitude.

From His very first encounter with Jesus, the desert

prophet got the impression that he had met the Master he sought. Jesus' insight into future events was so striking, His strength of character so self-evident, and His moral purity so absolute that when He asked John to baptize Him the latter at first refused, though finally he capitulated and did as Jesus requested.

When Jesus emerged from the green-slimed, sluggish water of the river Jordan, the bright heavens were opened to the Infinite, the breath of God blew upon His face, and He heard a voice that said: "Thou art My beloved Son, in whom I am well pleased."

Like the very first man, whom God fashioned from clay in Paradise, He received the life-giving spirit direct. He heard Himself addressed as the Son of God, a title which in bygone days the kings of Israel had assumed. By means of this mystical vision, experienced in a state of ecstasy, Jesus was celebrating His own kingly consecration. The ancient kings, however, did not connect their divine adoption with the moment of consecration; they knew it applied from the very moment any one of them was conceived. So it was with Jesus. His baptism only confirmed that natural bond, existing between Him and God, which lent such infinite richness to His inner life. In addition, this ritual act of initiation into the New Kingdom preached so fervently by John made Jesus feel more closely bound to humankind than ever before. ✴

John the Baptist baptized Jesus in the waters of the Jordan River; this event marked the beginning of Jesus' ministry. (Picturebank/H. Armstrong Roberts)

JESUS BANISHES THE TEMPTER

FULTON OURSLER

THE TEMPTATION

The Son of God,
Musing, and much revolving in
    His breast
How best the mighty work He
    might begin
Of Saviour to mankind, and which
    way first to
Publish His God-like office,
    now mature,
One day walked forth alone,
    the Spirit leading,
And His deep thoughts, the better
    to converse
With solitude; till far from track
    of men,
Thought following thought,
    and step by step led on
He entered now the bordering
    desert wild,
And, with dark shades and rocks
    environ'd round,
His holy meditations thus pursued
Sole, but with holiest meditations
    fed,
Into Himself descended, and at once
All His great work to come before
    Him set;
How to begin, how to accomplish
    best
His end of being on Earth,
    and mission high.

–JOHN MILTON

Telling no one what He intended to do, Jesus made His way alone into the wilderness. He was both led by the Spirit of God and driven by it, impelled and compelled to a great and lonely test. This parched and arid place was to be His place of testing; here, with red-tailed buzzards wheeling overhead, He was to endure a hideous experience none the less frightful because He deliberately invited the trial upon Himself.

On a hillside He found a cavern, and there He made His solitary camp. His sole reason for retreating to this grotto was that He must become acquainted with human suffering and temptation. He had to know them firsthand and altogether before He could begin His work. He must overcome temptation Himself—as a man, not as God—before He advised other men what they must do.

Here Jesus forced upon Himself a grueling discipline of fasting and solitude. For forty days He remained there eating nothing. And during those forty days, the little home in Nazareth and the blessed face of Mary His mother seemed very far away.

It was only after those forty weakening days and nights that Jesus was subject to the ordeal of temptation. Not until He was faint and exhausted did the temptations come—at a time when He felt weakest, most lonely, and friendless.

To Jesus were offered now all the beguilements and blandishments and cajoleries that have, since Eden, plagued the human race—uttered more often than not in quotations from the Scripture. Satan is a great repeater of God's words.

Why not abandon His great mission to help the suffering people? Why not think, instead, of Himself? After all, did the Son of God have to go on with this unnecessary farce? He who had the power to bring a feast ready to hand if He but gave the word! And another thing—why remain a lonely, obscure man, a carpenter about to turn wayside preacher? If the miraculous signs of His birth were to be trusted, then He had the power of God, and all the world would have to serve Him, and He would know such titanesque glory as no conqueror in history had ever known—not Darius, not Alexander, not Caesar. All mankind would adore Him. Why not?

His answer He drew from Scriptures of long ago: "The Lord, your God, shall you adore and Him only you shall serve—not in bread alone does man live, but in every word that proceeds out of the mouth of God. Get you behind Me, Satan!"

In His deliberately weakened condition, evil had not been easy to resist. No temptation ever is. But now Jesus, who in addition to being God was also a real man, had experienced the torments that come to men. And He had banished the temptations by the example of sheer devotion. ✄

This mountain, rising above the oasis city of Jericho, is believed to be the site where Jesus went up into the mountains and fasted and prayed for forty days, before being tempted by the devil. (Jeanne Conte)

THE END OF A PROPHET

EDGAR J. GOODSPEED

The few months of Jesus' active ministry are strangely interwoven with the work and fate of John the Baptist. It was the fame of John's preaching that had drawn Jesus from Nazareth to the Jordan thickets where John was thundering repentance and proclaiming a mightier one to come in judgment after him.

Jesus found John all He had anticipated and more. He said afterward to His own disciples, "I tell you, among men born of women no one has ever appeared greater than John the Baptist."

He had made the greatest friends of His life there in John's camp meetings by the Jordan—the men who afterward became His own first disciples and then the inner circle within the chosen band of the twelve. He found His own message and mission at His baptism and in the succeeding weeks of moral struggle in the wilderness. The initial impulse to begin to preach came to Jesus when, on returning to the scene of John's meetings, He had found the Baptist's followers gone and John himself hurried off to prison.

John had aroused the anger of Antipas when in his denunciation of the evils of the day he had pointed to the action of Antipas in putting away his lawful wife, the daughter of King Aretas of Arabia, and marrying Herodias. Even in prison Herodias wanted him put to death for this, but Antipas stood in awe of John and occasionally listened to what he had to say, though he found it very disturbing.

Herodias found her opportunity when in his birthday revels Antipas was entertaining his officers and courtiers, probably at his palace in Tiberias, which he had rebuilt in some splendor. In the course of this celebration, Herodias's

(photo, opposite page)
Jerash was one of the thriving cities of the Roman Decapolis when Jesus walked the earth. Now it is a city of ancient ruins.
(Jeanne Conte)

FOR THE BAPTIST

The last and greatest herald
  of Heaven's King,
Girt with rough skins, hies
  to the deserts wild,
Among that savage brood
  the woods forth bring,
Which he than man more
  harmless found and mild:
His food was blossoms, and
  what young doth spring,
With honey that from
  virgin hives distilled;
Parched body, hollow eyes,
  some uncouth thing
Made him appear, long since
  from Earth exiled.
There bust he forth; All ye,
  whose hopes rely
On God, with me
  amidst these deserts mourn,
Repent, repent, and from
  old errors turn.
Who listened to his voice,
  obeyed his cry?
    Only the echoes which
he made relent,
    Rung from their marble
caves, repent, repent.

—WILLIAM DRUMMOND OF
HAWTHORNDEN

daughter came in and, with entire disregard of her rank, gave a dance before the governor and his friends that so delighted him that he offered to give her anything she wanted.

After consulting her mother, she came back to the banquet hall and said to the governor, "I want John the Baptist's head on a platter!"

This horrible request sobered Antipas, but with all his boon companions about him he had not the courage to refuse, and he gave her what she asked. ▨

IV

THE MINISTRY OF JESUS

Now when Jesus had heard that John was cast into prison, He departed into Galilee; And leaving Nazareth, He came and dwelt in Capernaum, which is upon the sea coast, in the borders of Zabulon and Nephthalim: That it might be fulfilled which was spoken by Esaias the prophet. From that time Jesus began to preach, and to say, Repent: for the kingdom of heaven is at hand.   –MATTHEW 4:12–14, 17

THE CHOSEN

FULTON OURSLER

Again the next day after John stood, and two of his disciples; And looking upon Jesus as he walked, he saith, Behold the Lamb of God! And the two disciples heard him speak, and they followed Jesus.

–JOHN 1:35–37

The first step was to complete the selection of His principal followers who would be trained to carry forward His work when He would have to leave them.

Back in Capernaum He sent out Peter and James to bring to Him ten others whom He named from among the throng that helpfully and for months had followed Him wherever He went. An hour later, He arranged the Twelve in a circle around Him as they stood on an unfrequented part of the pebbly shore of the lake.

Bald and bearded Peter with his freckled nose was there, of course, and his tall brother Andrew. Near them stood the pale Bartholomew, who was also called Nathanael. Then came bright-eyed, impetuous John and his brother James, sons of Zebedee; and standing beside them was bearded Matthew, the exuberant ex-taxgatherer. Muscular, athletic Philip stood with his arm around the publican's shoulder. All these had been with the Master in His recent expeditions.

The others were newcomers. They had been selected from the large group of disciples who had followed the Master around Galilee.

First there was that other, younger James. Nearly forty years later, for love of Jesus, he was to be thrown down from the pinnacle of the Jerusalem Temple, and, being seen still to breathe, was finally to be stoned to death.

Standing with the younger James was the even younger Jude, his brother; Jude, who was called also Thaddeus and Lebbaeas; Jude, who would be regarded as obscure by future generations, after being shot to death by arrows in Armenia sixty years from this June day when he was chosen.

There was also Simon Zelotes, again a brother of young

(photo, pages 50–51)
The ruins of this synagogue are in Capernaum, near the Sea of Galilee. Capernaum was the site of many of Jesus' miracles, and He frequently taught in its synagogue. (R. Kord/H. Armstrong Roberts)

James and Jude. Simon was to be crucified at an appallingly old age; some say he was one hundred and twenty-nine years old when he was nailed to an X-like cross in Persia.

Among the last of those whom Jesus now selected was Thomas, surnamed Didymus but better known as doubting Thomas. Some later day in India he was to be ripped with a spear and die.

At the end of the list was Judas, the son of Simon of Kerioth. His name, Judas Iscariot, meant Judas of Kerioth.

A hybrid crew those twelve! Derived from incongruous sources! Yet Jesus informed them that He had chosen deliberately, and that His official mission must begin at once, with the death of John the Baptist. In the language of that day the term apostle meant "one who is sent" and was applied especially to couriers who carried letters from rulers or others in authority. Explicitly he named His Twelve as messengers. He would send them out to preach, promising that they, too, should heal sicknesses and cast out demons.

For a long time the thirteen stood in silent prayer, then started back into the town. Clearly, as they could see, He would need their devoted help. And the prospect was a little frightening; on that very day it seemed as if all the sick of the whole world were gathering in Capernaum.

Not without qualms the Apostles beheld the clamoring throngs. Soon it would be their job to heal such people. Life had, in so short a time, changed completely for these men. A little while ago they could have turned back, but no more. Jesus had chosen them, twelve and twelve only, as if in mystical recognition of the ancient tribes.

They followed Him, as He made His way along the shore, healing many along the way, until the press of people grew so large that once again He took refuge in a fisherman's boat. The time had come when He and His chosen must put the multitudes off from them and be alone together. ✷

JESUS PRAYING

And it came to pass in those days, that He went out into a mountain to pray, and continued all night in prayer to God. And when it was day, He called unto Him His disciples: and of them He chose twelve, whom also He named apostles.

–LUKE 6:12–13

He sought the mountain and the
    loneliest height,
For He would meet His Father
    all alone,
And there, with many a tear and
    many a groan,
He strove in prayer throughout the
    long, long night.
Why need He pray, who held by
    filial right,
O'er all the world alike of thought
    and sense,
The fulness of his Sire's omnipotence?
Why crave in prayer what was His
    own by might?
Vain is the question—Christ was man
    in need,
And being man His duty was to pray.
The Son of God confess'd the
    human need,
And doubtless ask'd a blessing
    every day.
Nor ceases yet for sinful man to please,
Nor will, till heaven and earth shall
    pass away.

–HARTLEY COLERIDGE

TWO BROTHERS FROM CAPERNAUM

NORMAN VINCENT PEALE

In this dramatic interpretation of the life of Jesus, Dr. Peale tells the story from the point of view of Joshua, a young man who lived near Capernaum. In this excerpt, Joshua and his friend, Benhaded, who did not believe in Jesus, have followed the group of men who will soon become the first disciples.

And Jesus, walking by the sea of Galilee, saw two brethren, Simon called Peter, and Andrew his brother, casting a net into the sea: for they were fishers. And He saith unto them, Follow Me, and I will make you fishers of men. And they straightway left their nets, and followed Him.

–MATTHEW 4:18–20

A group of men from Capernaum followed Jesus whenever possible. Andrew, my father, and my Uncle Simon, whom Jesus called Peter, were two of His most devoted disciples. Many of us younger people went along for the excitement. Benhaded, too, accompanied us from time to time, to listen and laugh at the man he called a fool.

The common people admired Jesus, for He had a fascinating way of talking, so simple and calm. Yet the things He said were so different that the mind became excited and something deep within responded.

Jesus often sat and talked to His followers in the afternoon shade, with everyone grouped about Him on the grass. But I liked it better in the evenings when only His disciples were with Him. I could look at the bright stars above and listen and really think. I found pleasure in watching the faces of the disciples with the firelight reflected upon them. In that inner circle sat the twelve men whom Jesus had especially selected to instruct, because, as Uncle Simon explained, you cannot trust the bigger crowd to understand. There must be a chosen few whose loyalty is unquestioned.

Jesus was popular with the people. So many of them were stirred by His new ideas of love, brotherhood, and God. But He had enemies. It was rumored that two groups especially were out to destroy Him: the scribes, our lawyers, who do not believe in the creative force of spiritual things; and the Pharisees, our puritanical churchmen, who oppose all prophets. Jesus wanted to be sure His teachings would live on. Therefore, He needed men who were strong and wise enough to take over after His death. He chose them well.

His disciples are strong individualists, thinkers, leaders. Among them are fishermen and students, mathematicians and tax collectors. They were all disturbed by the unfair conditions imposed upon them by both state and church. There was so little to satisfy the spiritual needs and longings of men. There was an emptiness, and men sought for inner peace and, even more, for the certainty that life has meaning. In Jesus, the disciples seemed to have found an answer. It was hard for me to describe to Benhaded what I saw in Jesus and in the faces of His men around Him, for it is beyond my comprehension. But I sense that they have discovered something that is deeply satisfying. And I long for such satisfaction within myself.

THE SHIP IN THE MIDST OF THE SEA

The waters were Thy path;
   Thy way was on the sea:
Who in that night could trace
    Thy steps?
   Who solve the mystery?

Some at Capernaum asked,
   "When and how cam'st Thou
   here?"
In vain they tried to find the
   track
   By which Thou didst appear.

But Thy disciples, Lord,
   Did gladly Thee receive;
And then the ship was at the
   shore:
   They pry not, but believe.

Lord, in Thy sacraments
   Thou walkest on the sea;
Let us not ask, "How dost Thou
   come?"
   But gladly welcome Thee.

Then will the winds be hushed,
   The waves no longer roar;
When Christ is with us in the
   ship,
   The ship is at the shore.

   —CHRISTOPHER
    WORDSWORTH, D.D.

The people of Capernaum did not follow Jesus, despite His frequent presence in the city. He cursed the city for its disbelief and predicted its ruin—a prophecy that came all too true. (Jeanne Conte)

FROM IMMANENCE

I come in the little things,
Saith the Lord:
My starry wings
I do forsake,
Love's highway of humility to take:
Meekly I fit my stature to your need.
In beggar's part
About your gates I shall not cease
    to plead—
As man, to speak with man—
Till by such art
I shall achieve My Immemorial Plan,
Pass the low lintel of the
    human heart.

—EVELYN UNDERHILL

WORDS OF MEANING

DALLAS LORE SHARP

As a form of illustration the parable was very common among Jewish teachers, but Jesus so spiritualized and perfected it, that parabolic teaching may rightly be called the creation of Jesus—a way He had of teaching spiritual truth. It consisted in taking some incident of life or nature, or some imaginary narrative whose truth and commonness was instantly recognized, and making this the foundation of moral and spiritual teaching.

But let us return to the seashore and take our place, not with the multitude on the beach, but with the Twelve in the boat. Beyond the crowd upon the shore, in the distance, was a sower, going back and forth across his field in the fertile plain of Gennesaret, scattering the seed of his fall planting.

Pointing silently to the sower, till everyone in the throng was gazing in expectant curiosity upon him, Jesus began to speak with strange significance, but with strangely hidden meaning: "The sower went forth to sow." The parable of the sower! The first such discourse they had ever heard from Jesus! What did it mean?

We have always known the Master's explanation, and to us the meaning is as clear as morning light. But to those who listened that day, except to those who saw in Jesus the Divine Sower and who saw in His words the good seed, it was all a mystery. These crowds flocked about Jesus to hear what He had to say about the kingdom of God so long promised; and while a few believed Him the promised Messiah about to establish this kingdom, both unbelieving crowds and believing followers were alike mistaken in the nature of the kingdom, and the way it should come, so that while the multitudes found this parable a total mystery, the disciples, even, had to ask its complete meaning. All were still looking for a material kingdom, a Messiah who would be an earthly King and establish His power by force. But no. He had indeed brought the kingdom—a kingdom not to be *about* them but *within* them. Their hearts were its soil; He the sower; His gospel the seed.

It was perhaps while the multitudes were discussing the meaning of these mysterious words that the disciples in the boat asked and received of Jesus His explanation of the parable. How altogether different this idea from their Jewish notions! Not outward, of sudden and splendid conquest, but inward, of slow growth; not by might, but by spirit!

Again He addressed the people. He had just told them how the kingdom came, or how it was planted; now He advances a step in the development of the kingdom, and with the parable of the growing seed (Mark 4:26) tells them how the kingdom grows. It grows as a seed grows. The farmer sows it, and that is all he can do; but while he attends to his ordinary duties, the earth, with life-giving power within herself, brings the seed from leaf to ripened fruit. The farmer sees the growth, even reaps the grain, but cannot tell how it grew. So he, the Sower, will drop the seed and leave it to the quickening, developing power inherent in the seed and in the soil and in the showers until the harvest is ripe. Darker and darker grew the "mystery of the kingdom" to those "without"; clearer and clearer it grew to those who, in sympathy and belief, were already within the kingdom.

But still the mystery was to be made more mysterious or made wholly plain. In that country then and to this day it is no uncommon thing for an enemy to come in the night, and upon a man's field of newly planted wheat, to sow tares. These tares, according to Jewish legend, were a degenerate poisonous kind of wheat, indistinguishable from good wheat until it came to seed. The kingdom is like a

WHAT WENT YE OUT FOR TO SEE?

Across the sea, along the shore,
In numbers more and ever more,
From lonely hut and busy town,
The valley through, the
    mountain down,
What was it ye went out to see,
Ye silly folk of Galilee?
The reeds that in the wind
    doth shake?
The weed that washes in the lake?
The reeds that waver, the weeds
    that float?
A young man preaching in a boat. . . .

A prophet? Boys and women weak!
    Declare, or cease to rave;
Whence is it He hath learned to speak?
    Say, who His doctrine gave?
A prophet? Prophet wherefore He
    Of all in Israel tribes?
He teacheth with authority,
    And not as do the scribes.

–A. H. CLOUGH

THE SOWER

Ye sons of earth prepare the plough,
    Break up your fallow ground!
The Sower is gone forth to sow
    And scatter blessings round.

The seed that finds a stony soil
    Shoots forth a hasty blade;
But ill repays the sower's toil,
    Soon withered, scorched, and
        dead.

The thorny ground is sure to balk
    All hopes of harvest there;
We find a tall and sickly stalk,
    But not the fruitful ear.

The beaten path and high-way side
    Receive the trust in vain;
The watchful birds the spoil divide
    And pick up all the grain.

But where the Lord of grace and
        power
    Has blessed the happy field;
How plenteous is the golden store
    The deep-wrought furrows
        yield!

Father of mercies, we have need
    Of Thy preparing grace;
Let the same hand that gives
        the seed
    Provide a fruitful place.

–WILLIAM COWPER

field of wheat oversown with tares. All understood the picture, but not even the disciples saw its application to the conditions in the kingdom. It was necessary for the disciples to learn this lesson now, for already in the kingdom, among their own numbers, were tares—the sowing of Satan, that must grow together until the harvest, when, without harm, the separation can be made.

Three more un-Jewish pictures of the kingdom could not have been drawn to illustrate the mystery of the kingdom. But Jesus had not ended His teaching. Two more perfect pictures of the kingdom He now drew for them, neither of which they could then understand, for they could not conceive of the kingdom in any such lights. First, with the parable of the mustard-seed, Jesus told how the kingdom, from the smallest, most insignificant beginnings, would grow outward and extend itself until it became greater than all other realms of spiritual truth; and how the nations would rest in it as birds settled among the wide-spreading branches of the mustard plant, which grew to be the greatest garden herb from the smallest garden seed. Then with that other homely parable of meal and leaven He illustrated how the kingdom, being hidden in a man's or a nation's heart, grew inward, pervading and transforming the whole life.

The multitudes were dismissed and Jesus with His disciples returned to His house in Capernaum.

The day was nearly done, yet Jesus had some further private words for His followers. All they had heard today was about the kingdom. But the kingdom was not something to be taught only—it was a reality, a gift, to be valued and possessed; and with two more parables—the treasure hid in the field, and the pearl of great price—the Master showed them how great and how priceless a treasure it was, and what they must give up to have it.

The twilight lay in long shadows upon the shore and

over the sleeping lake. Jesus went out in the clear, cool evening to rest by the seaside, but His very appearance in the streets was heralded. Turning to the disciples He said, "Let us depart to the other side of the sea." The disciples, in their eagerness to escape, hurried into the boat without forethought or provision and pushed off.

But while this was being done, a Jewish scribe, dazzled by the marvelous teaching of Jesus, and feeling that Jesus would surely need and accept one so learned and authoritative as himself, exclaimed, "Master, I will follow Thee whithersoever Thou goest."

But Jesus, seeing into the man that he was like the stony soil, whereon the seed had sprouted quickly, but would quickly wither, replied: "Foxes have holes, and the birds of the air have nests; but the Son of man hath no where to lay His head."

A small sailboat on the Sea of Galilee.
(Zefa/H. Armstrong Roberts)

That discouraging fact was enough for the scribe; he was neither received nor rejected—simply tested. We never hear of him again.

Then an earnest listener, who now would become a regular follower, seeing the hasty departure said, "Lord, suffer me first to go and bury my father."

"Follow Me," was the startling and unconditional command of Jesus, "and let the dead bury their dead"—by which He meant, Let those who are dead to My truth attend to those worldly cares. 🔲

And it came to pass, when Jesus had ended these sayings, the people were astonished at His doctrine.

–MATTHEW 7:28

ON THE HOLY SCRIPTURES

Why did our blessed Savior please
    to break
His sacred thoughts in parables;
    and speak
In dark enigmas? Whosoe'er thou be
That findst them so, they were not
    spoke to thee:
In what a case is he, that haps to run
Against a post, and cries,
    How dark's the sun?
Or he, in summer, that complains
    of frost?
The Gospel's hid to none, but who
    are lost:
The Scripture is a ford, wherein,
    'tis said,
An elephant shall swim; a lamb
    may wade.

–FRANCIS QUARLES

TWO PARABLES FOR CHILDREN

CHARLES DICKENS

In this story written for his children, Charles Dickens recounts in his own words two of the well-known parables that Jesus taught.

And He told His disciples this story—He said,

"There was once a servant who owed his master a great deal of money and could not pay it. At which the master, being very angry, was going to have this servant sold for a slave. But the servant, kneeling down and begging his master's pardon with great sorrow, the master forgave him. Now this same servant had a fellow servant who owed him a hundred pence, and instead of being kind and forgiving to this poor man, as his master had been to him, he put him in prison for the debt. His master, hearing of it, went to him and said, 'O wicked servant, I forgave you. Why did you not forgive your fellow servant?' And because he had not done so, his master turned him away with great misery. So," said our Saviour, "how can you expect God to forgive you, if you do not forgive others? This is the meaning of that part of the Lord's Prayer, where we say 'Forgive us our trespasses'—that word means faults—'as we forgive them that trespass against us.'"

And He told them another story, and said: "There was a certain farmer once, who had a yard, and he went out early in the morning, and agreed with some laborers to work there, all day, for a penny. And by and by, when it was later, he went out again and engaged some more laborers on the same terms; and by and by went out again; and so on, several times, until the afternoon. When the day was over, and they all came to be paid, those who had worked since morning complained that those who had not begun to work until late in the day had the same money as themselves, and they said it was not fair. But the master said,

'Friend, I agreed with you for a penny; and is it less money to you, because I give the same money to another man?'"

Our Saviour meant to teach them by this, that people who have done good all their lives long will go to Heaven after they are dead. But that people who have been wicked, because of their being miserable, or not having parents and friends to take care of them when young, and who are truly sorry for it, however late in their lives, and pray God to forgive them, will be forgiven and will go to Heaven too. He taught His disciples in these stories, because He knew the people liked to hear them, and would remember what He said better, if He said it in that way. ▨

Although no one knows exactly where Jesus taught His disciples the Lord's Prayer, it could have been here among the trees of the Mount of Olives where the Church of Pater Noster *now stands to commemorate this moment.* (Jeanne Conte)

THE MASTER TEACHER

GRACE NOLL CROWELL

The Jews believed that one important characteristic of the Messiah would be that He should be able to tell them all things, even the secrets of their hearts. They evidently gained this conception from the eleventh chapter of Isaiah: "There shall come forth a rod out of Jesse . . . and the spirit of the LORD shall rest upon Him, the spirit of wisdom and understanding, the spirit of counsel and might, the spirit of knowledge and of the fear of the LORD."

Nicodemus was a man carrying a load of grave responsibilities. The Jews depended upon him for his counsel and advice, and he had probably run into problems that he was unable to solve at this particular hour. He needed help and instruction, and whom should he seek other than the great Teacher of all time, who was drawing men to Himself by the thousands with His wisdom and understanding?

Nicodemus came to Jesus by night, probably not so much through fear of the Jews as through a desire to meet the man alone so they could discuss his problems uninterrupted. Nicodemus had witnessed Him daily, surrounded by vast multitudes, and there seemed no opportunity for him to speak quietly with Jesus. This he so much longed to do.

Nicodemus respected the man, but apparently he had no intention of being one of His disciples. He was seeking Him with a selfish motive as men so often do today. He addressed Him as Rabbi, which means divine teacher, or master. This was a straightforward acknowledgment of his respect and belief in the man whom he was addressing.

Even then, the Jewish leader did not get to discuss his personal problems. The Teacher took advantage of the would-be questioner and at once delved into things eternal.

In that brief conversation were condensed all the important truths of time and eternity. Nicodemus's spiritual education could have been complete through the instruction he received that day if he had been receptive, and who can say—perhaps he was. At any rate he went away thoughtfully, his own problems shrunken into insignificance before the vast understanding of the man called Jesus.

We recall that before Christ chose the twelve men who were to be His disciples, He spent the entire night upon a mountainside in prayer. The following day was to be an especially important one in His early ministry. He was seeking counsel of His Father, and we may be certain He received it.

He was to begin some important teaching on the following day. He was to deliver at least a portion of what has been known through the centuries as the Sermon on the Mount.

What He was to say, He realized, would go down through the ages to countless ones yet unborn. The twelve men He had chosen to follow Him were with Him as He descended to meet the waiting multitude. Luke tells us that He "came down to the plain"; Matthew speaks of His "going up into a mountain." Doubtless it was a slight eminence that He climbed in order to look out upon the sea of faces as He delivered the greatest dissertation in history.

It was an instructive lesson, and He was the instructor. His listeners—many of them from Judaea and Jerusalem, many from Tyre and Sidon—had come from everywhere to hear Him speak as well as to be healed of their diseases.

Jesus sat down to deliver His address; it was the posture of the teachers in that day.

On the northwest shore of the Sea, or Lake, of Galilee lies the slope where Jesus is believed to have delivered the Sermon on the Mount. (Jeanne Conte)

Saviour, Teach Me Day by Day

Saviour, teach me day by day,
Love's sweet lesson to obey;
Sweeter lesson cannot be—
Loving Him who first loved me.

With a childlike heart of love,
At Thy bidding may I move;
Prompt to serve and follow Thee—
Loving Him who first loved me.

Teach me all Thy steps to trace,
Strong to follow in Thy grace;
Learning how to love from Thee—
Loving Him who first loved me.

Love in loving finds employ,
In obedience all her joy;
Ever new that joy will be—
Loving Him who first loved me.

—Jane E. Leeson

(photo opposite)
It is believed that Jesus delivered the Sermon on the Mount here on the Mount of the Beatitudes, near Tabgha and Bethsaida and on the northwest shore of the Sea of Galilee.
(Erich Lessing/Art Resource)

And there He lifted up His eyes and His voice and began preaching His never-to-be-forgotten sermon.

What a revelation His strongly moving weighty words must have been to that curious waiting throng! Surely they could not have forgotten them their lifetime through. Those words are still a vital part of living for every lover of the Christ. His blessing ascends from them for the pure in heart, for the merciful, for the meek, for the peacemakers, for all sorrowing and persecuted ones.

Here is a map of behavior. It is a guidepost for everyday living. Should one follow the road there pointed out by the hand of the living God, none would be lost, none would come short of the glory that awaits the pilgrims of the earth.

The text of the sermon may well be considered the firm, strong foundation upon which to build our house of life. God grant that we may turn often to the carefully stenciled blueprint in order that our houses may stand unshaken and secure against the evil winds of life.

In the sixth chapter of Matthew, Christ is still teaching. It likely is a continuation of the Sermon on the Mount. Here He is giving instructions on almsgiving, on forgiveness, on the laying up of treasures; and He gives therein that glowing example for men to follow as they pray. The Lord's Prayer was taught that day to poor, seeking, groping mankind who knows not how to pray except they be taught.

The very air of the mountainside must have been rife with the sound of those deathless words. They are still caught and held by unseen aerials and transmitted to us across the centuries. The reception is crystal-clear. The meaning is plain for us to hear and heed.

Oh, the wonder of it! Oh, the might and power of a voice still speaking after all the years, bidding us look homeward, bidding us find unhindered the way He has prepared for us.

THE SERMON ON THE MOUNT

MATTHEW 5:1–19

Above the Lake of Galilee
Soft winds are blowing still,
With lyric words of love set free
Above the Lake of Galilee.
They blow across the timeless sea,
Immortal words that thrill.
Above the Lake of Galilee
Soft winds are blowing still.

—ALINE BADGER CARTER

And seeing the multitudes, He went up into a mountain: and when He was set, His disciples came unto Him: And He opened His mouth, and taught them, saying,

Blessed are the poor in spirit: for theirs is the kingdom of heaven.

Blessed are they that mourn: for they shall be comforted.

Blessed are the meek: for they shall inherit the earth.

Blessed are they which do hunger and thirst after righteousness: for they shall be filled.

Blessed are the merciful: for they shall obtain mercy.

Blessed are the pure in heart: for they shall see God.

Blessed are the peacemakers: for they shall be called the children of God.

Blessed are they which are persecuted for righteousness' sake: for theirs is the kingdom of heaven.

Blessed are ye, when men shall revile you, and persecute you, and shall say all manner of evil against you falsely, for My sake.

Rejoice, and be exceeding glad: for great is your reward in heaven: for so persecuted they the prophets which were before you.

Ye are the salt of the earth: but if the salt have lost his savour, wherewith shall it be salted? it is thenceforth good for nothing, but to be cast out, and to be trodden under foot of men.

Ye are the light of the world. A city that is set on an hill cannot be hid.

Neither do men light a candle, and put it under a bushel, but on a candlestick; and it giveth light unto all that are in the house.

Let your light so shine before men, that they may see your good works, and glorify your Father which is in heaven.

Think not that I am come to destroy the law, or the prophets: I am not come to destroy, but to fulfill.

For verily I say unto you, Till heaven and earth pass, one jot or one tittle shall in no wise pass from the law, till all be fulfilled.

Whosoever therefore shall break one of these least commandments, and shall teach men so, he shall be called the least in the kingdom of heaven: but whosoever shall do and teach them, the same shall be called great in the kingdom of heaven. ✸

Whereas the actual site of the Sermon on the Mount cannot be verified, a church has been built on the spot traditionally identified as the Mount of the Beatitudes. (R. Kord/H. Armstrong Roberts)

THE LORD'S PRAYER

ROGER L. SHINN

After this manner therefore pray
ye: Our Father which art in
heaven, Hallowed be Thy name.
Thy kingdom come. Thy will be
done in earth, as it is in heaven.
Give us this day our daily bread.
And forgive us our debts, as we
forgive our debtors. And lead us
not into temptation, but deliver
us from evil: For Thine is the
kingdom, and the power, and the
glory, for ever. Amen.
–MATTHEW 6:9–13

Few prayers are shorter or use simpler language than the Lord's Prayer. Yet the words carry a weight of meaning from the whole gospel. We see this when we examine the petitions.

"Our Father who art in heaven." Augustine says that the opening words are already the answer to the prayer, for we can ask nothing greater than to approach the Lord of the universe as Father.

"Thy kingdom come, Thy will be done." The phrases are both petitions and expressions of trust. They call on God, who alone can establish His kingdom. And they call on the praying person to conform to the will of God.

The heart of the prayer, "Thy kingdom come," is the heart of Jesus' whole message. He bids His disciples pray for that work of God, already beginning but not yet complete.

Although the kingdom is a gift of God, its practical significance for us is clear in the petition, "Thy will be done in earth as it is in heaven." The citizens of God's heavenly kingdom are called to live by God's will on earth. That should be the normal expectation of any religious commitment. Here it is a call to daring life.

"Give us this day our daily bread." Immediately the prayer turns from the exalted to the commonplace. What is so common as daily bread? To pray for bread—for oneself and the world—is as basic to the Christian as to pray, "Hallowed be Thy name."

"Forgive us our debts." Anyone who has read the Sermon on the Mount up to this point will not be surprised by the prayer for forgiveness. Once again we see that the New Covenant is a covenant of grace. We meet its terms not by perfect compliance with God's will, but by accepting in faith His forgiveness.

This faith will prompt us to forgive. In Matthew, the prayer is followed by the foreboding words of verses 14–15. The idea is not that God is only as generous as we are. The gospel often refutes that idea. But if we refuse to forgive, we lack the faith that can accept forgiveness.

"Lead us not into temptation." Does a good God deliberately tempt us? If He wants to test us, should we pray that He not do so?

Here, as in other sayings of Jesus, we can get help from the scholars who translate the Greek back into the probable Aramaic words of Jesus. Then the sentence means: "Do not allow us to be led into temptation." Or: "Do not let us be tested beyond our capacity to endure." God is not the tempter, but He has put us into a world of temptations.

In this world we may prayerfully seek to avoid temptations. But what is more important, we pray that we shall not yield to them, that God will deliver us from the evils into which we might be tempted.

Christians often conclude the Lord's Prayer with the words: "For Thine is the kingdom and the power and the glory, for ever. Amen."

This final doxology or paean of praise does not appear in the oldest manuscripts of the New Testament. By the second century, we know, Christians were using it widely. It echoes earlier themes in the prayer: it hallows God's name and it ascribes to Him lordship in His kingdom.

Amen means *truly, verily,* or *may it certainly be so.* When Christians end this prayer with a genuine Amen, they glorify God. While the church has often drawn up creeds to define loyalty, Christ gave His followers a prayer rather than a creed. Christians, separated by doctrines and ecclesiastical authorities, are able to unite in this prayer. That is appropriate, since the prayer comes from Christ Himself.

Ensamples of Our Saviour

Our Saviour
    (Paterne of true holinesse)
Continuall praid
    Us by ensample teaching,

When He was baptized
    In the wildernesse,
In working miracles
    And in His preaching,

Upon the mount
    In garden grones of death,
At His last Supper,
    At His parting breath.

O fortresse of the faithfull,
    Sure defence,
In which doth Christians'
    Cognizance consist:

Nothing more gratefull
    In the Highest eyes,
Nothing more firme
    In danger to protect us,

Nothing more forcible
    To pierce the skies,
And not depart
    Till mercy doe respect us;

And as the soule
    Life to the body gives,
So prayer revives
    The soule, by prayer it lives.

—Robert Southwell

THE BOY WHO SAW JESUS

EDWARD WAGENKNECHT

Andrew was a little Jewish boy who lived, very many years ago, in Palestine, in a small city called Tiberias. He lived with his father, Reuben, who was a fisherman, and two older brothers, Joseph and Judas.

Andrew and his father and his brothers were very poor, but that was not what made the little boy unhappy. He was unhappy because he was lonely.

It was just about this time that Andrew began to hear about a wonderful man who was coming to be talked about around the Sea of Galilee. His name was Joshua, or, as the Greeks had it, Jesus. He spent all His time going about the country helping people.

Nobody knew where this Jesus of Nazareth had got His strange power. At Capernaum He had done many wonderful things. He could heal sick people, it seemed, simply by placing His hands upon them. Even stranger stories than this were told of Him. It was said that He had once walked on the water as calmly, as confidently, as men walk on dry land. It was said He had once fed a hungry crowd with five loaves and two little fishes.

Andrew did not doubt for a moment that He might have done it. But it did not matter much whether He had done it or not. It was not because Jesus had walked on the water that Andrew loved Him.

For he did love Him. It had come to that. The little boy was in love with a man he had never seen.

He came, one night at sunset, down the shore of the lake, on foot, with His chosen disciples about Him, a poor man, poorly dressed, His robe covered with the dust of His journey.

The news spread quickly throughout Tiberias.

Many people went down to the seashore to meet Jesus as He came into Tiberias, but very few of them loved Him. Nearly all of them wanted something.

When Andrew arrived, the Teacher was sitting on a stone by the seashore, talking quietly to those who had gathered about Him. The boy had imagined Him in a thousand different ways, each more wonderful than the last, but nothing that he had imagined was half so wonderful as what he saw. There was such strength and such loveliness in the Teacher's face that it seemed as if all the beauty and all the goodness in the world were centered there. His father's commands meant nothing to him now, nor did he care that he was making a fool of himself. He did what in all his brooding over the Teacher's coming he had never once dared to imagine himself doing: he rushed forward and cast himself at Jesus' feet, his arms around the Master's knees.

Not even Reuben had expected that. He was more angry than he had ever been in his life.

He came forward quickly, and his respect for the presence of Jesus could only just barely keep the harsh word on his lips from turning into an oath. He seized his son roughly by one arm and dragged him to his feet.

Jesus rose with the boy. He knew that when men do wrong it is either because they cannot see the light or because they lack the courage to follow it. But the hand that Reuben had raised to strike his son never descended.

"Suffer little children," He said (Reuben was never to forget His words), "suffer little children to come unto Me, and forbid them not; for of such is the kingdom of God. Verily I say unto you, whosoever shall not receive the kingdom of God as a little child, shall in no wise enter therein."

"I thought . . . " began the embarrassed father, "I only meant . . . "

But Jesus continued, more sternly than before: "Take

THE CHILDREN WHOM JESUS BLESSED

Happy were they, the mothers, in
    whose sight
Ye grew, fair children! hallowed
    from that hour
By your Lord's blessing. Surely thence
    a shower
Of heavenly beauty, a transmitted
    light
Hung on your brows and eyelids,
    meekly bright,
Through all the after years, which saw
    ye move
Lowly, yet still majestic, in the might,
The conscious glory of the
    Saviour's love!
And honored be all childhood,
    for the sake
Of that high love! Let reverential care
Watch to behold the immortal
    spirit wake,
And shield its first bloom from
    unholy air;
Owning, in each young suppliant
    glance, the sign
Of claims upon a heritage Divine.

—FELICIA DOROTHEA HEMANS

heed that you despise not one of these little ones; for I say unto you that in heaven their angels do always behold the face of My Father which is in heaven."

What need is there that I should write any more? If you have followed my story thus far, you know how Andrew felt as the Master spoke these words quite as well as I could tell you.

He was always thereafter faithful to Jesus. He was too young to become one of His disciples, that day in Tiberias,

though he would dearly have loved to do so, but in later years, after the Teacher had died, he was among the faithful who helped to carry on His work. His life, not so important as the world counts importance, was built into the very fabric of the Christian Church. Jesus won his heart, that day by the seashore, for time and for eternity. The Master vindicated the boy, and the boy gave the Master the opportunity to utter one of the most gracious sayings that ever fell from His lips. ✷

It is not known whether Jesus ever visited Tiberias, although He traveled in the area and likely attracted followers from this small city in Galilee. (R. Kord/H. Armstrong Roberts)

A LESSON OF FORGIVENESS

FULTON SHEEN

While visiting the Galilean towns early in His public life and before open hostility had broken out, a rich Pharisee named Simon invited Our Lord to his home for a meal. He had heard of the acclaim given Our Lord by the people and was anxious to determine for himself whether He was really a prophet or a teacher.

When Our Lord arrived, there was little enthusiasm in the welcome of Simon who coldly omitted the usual courtesies and attentions paid to a guest. Perhaps Simon knew he was watched by other Pharisees and hence omitted these courtesies.

While the meal was being served, an untoward incident happened. Simon looked up, and what he saw brought a blush to his cheek. He would not have minded it if anyone else had been there, but This Man! What would He think of it? The intruder was a woman; her name was Mary; her profession, a sinner, a common woman of the streets. She stood at the feet of Our Blessed Lord and let fall upon those sandaled harbingers of peace, like the first drops of warm summer rain, a few tears. Then, ashamed of what she had done, she bent lower as if to hide her shame, but the fountain of tears would not be stilled. Emboldened because unreproved, she cast herself on her knees and began to wipe the tears from His feet with her long disheveled hair. To anoint the head was the usual course, but she would not venture on such an honor but would make bold in her humility to anoint only His feet. Taking from her veil a vessel of precious perfume, she did not pour it out drop by drop, slowly, as if to indicate by the very slowness of giving the generosity of the giver. She broke the vessel and gave everything, for love knows no limits. There was love in her boldness, repentance in her tears, sacrifice and surrender of self in her ointment.

But the Pharisee was horrified that the Master should have allowed such a disreputable woman of the streets to approach Him, and contrary to all traditions of the strict Pharisees, to pour out tears at His feet. Simon would not speak the words aloud, but merely thought within himself: If this fellow were a real prophet, He would know who this woman is that touches Him, and what sort of woman she is: a sinner.

Our Lord then read Simon's thoughts as He will one day read the souls of the living and the dead. He said to him: "Simon, I have something to say to you."

Simon said: "Speak on, Master."

Our Lord continued: "Two men were in debt to a moneylender: one owed him five hundred silver pieces, the other fifty. As neither had anything to pay with, he let them both off. Now, which will love him most?"

Simon replied, "I should think the one that was let off most."

"You are right," said Jesus. Then turning to the woman, He said to Simon, "You see this woman? I came to your house: you provided no water for My feet; but this woman has made My feet wet with her tears and wiped them with her hair. You gave Me no kiss; but she has been kissing My feet ever since I came in. You did not anoint My head with oil; but she has anointed My feet with myrrh."

"She has washed My feet with tears. And so, I tell you, her great love proves that her many sins have been forgiven; where little has been forgiven, little love is shown."

Simon had something to learn, so he invited a teacher; the woman had something to be forgiven, so she poured out her contrite tears.

The lesson was over and the woman was dismissed with the words: Your sins are forgiven.

WERE NOT THE SINFUL MARY'S TEARS

Were not the sinful Mary's tears
An offering worthy Heaven,
When o'er the faults of former years
She wept—and was forgiven?

When bringing every balmy sweet
Her day of luxury stored,
She o'er her Saviour's hallow'd feet
The precious perfume pour'd;

And wiped them with that
golden hair
Where once the diamonds shone,
Though now those gems of grief
were there
Which shine for God alone.

Were not those sweets, though
humbly shed,
That hair—those weeping eyes—
And the sunk heart that inly bled—
Heaven's noblest sacrifice?

Thou that hast slept in error's sleep,
Oh! wouldst thou wake in heaven,
Like Mary kneel, like Mary weep,
"Love much," and be forgiven?

—THOMAS MOORE

JESUS IN THE SYNAGOGUE

PEARL S. BUCK

And Jesus returned in the power of the Spirit into Galilee: and there went out a fame of Him through all the region round about. And He taught in their synagogues, being glorified of all.

And He came to Nazareth, where He had been brought up: and, as His custom was, He went into the synagogue on the sabbath day, and stood up for to read.

And Jesus returned in the power of the Spirit into Galilee: and there went out a fame of Him through all the region round about. And He taught in their synagogues, being glorified of all.

And He came to Nazareth, where He had been brought up: and, as His custom was, He went into the synagogue on the sabbath day, and stood up for to read.

–LUKE 4:14–16

This tiny little synagogue stands in Nazareth—a bit below ground as any site would be after 2,000 years. Visitors walk down seven steep steps to this arched stone-walled place of worship which has been traced to the time of Christ. (Jeanne Conte)

The synagogue was crowded with the curious and devout, and there was silence as He stood up and opened the book written by the prophet Isaiah hundreds of years before. He found the place He sought, and read:

"The Spirit of the Lord is upon Me,
Because He has anointed Me to preach the gospel to the poor;
He has sent Me to heal the broken-hearted,
To preach deliverance to the captives,
And recovery of sight to the blind,
To set at liberty those that are bruised,
And to preach the chosen year of the Lord."

He closed the book and gave it back to the attendant, and then sat down to explain the meaning of the passage whose words they already knew so well. They knew that it referred to the Messiah. But they did not know when this Messiah was to come or what He would be like, although they did expect Him to be a conquering king.

His next words astonished them.

He said: "Today has this scripture been fulfilled in your ears."

At first they did not realize what He meant. But then they stirred and whispered to each other, wondering at His words. For He had said that He was the one of whom the prophet had written, that *He* was the Son of God!

They looked at Him resentfully. He was a healer and a teacher, yes, and perhaps a prophet; but still He was only their neighbor, only the son of a carpenter, only a man born on earth like all the rest of them. Now He was suggesting that He was the Messiah, the King and Savior of the Jews!

Jesus knew that they did not believe in Him, that they would expect Him to perform some feat before their very eyes to prove His words. But that was not the nature of His teaching.

So Jesus said to them: "You will surely say to Me, 'Physician, heal Your own. What we have heard You to have done in Capernaum, do also in Your own country.' But I say to you, no prophet is accepted in his own country or by his own people. There were many widows in Israel in the days of Elijah, when the heavens were shut for three years and six months so that no rain fell and there was famine in the land. But they did not believe in him; to none of them was he sent by the Lord. And there were many lepers in Israel at the time of Elisha the prophet. None of them were cleansed, for they did not believe. But Naaman the Syrian was cured of his leprosy, for he believed and sought Elisha's help. And, like the people of Israel in those days, *you* do not believe!"

All the people in the synagogue were filled with wrath when they heard Him say these things. Their admiration turned to sudden hatred and they rose up, shouting with rage. To this sort of teaching, to these words from a fellow Nazarene of all people, they surely would not listen! They laid rough hands on Him and thrust Him out of the synagogue and out of the city of Nazareth. Then they led Him to the top of the craggy hill upon which the city was built so that they might cast Him headlong over the side of it. Somehow He escaped them. They did not even notice until they were on the hilltop and ready to throw Him down onto the rocks below that He had passed quietly through their midst and gone along His way.

THEIR MESSIAH REJECTED

Predictions filled and
　　wonders wrought
Proved Christ to be the Savior sought,
Who better things to men had
　　brought.

Deliverance the Jews await,
Yet cast aside their Savior great,
Through pride, through envy, and
　　through hate.

The Jews expected Christ to be
A conqueror in high degree,
Whom everyone should wish to see.

But Jesus spoke to them no lies—
Not David's kingdom would He rise,
But one all nations to comprise.

The Jews would not to Him attend,
Were loath allegiance to lend
To one so low, the poor man's friend.

When He appeared as of the poor,
His presence they could not endure,
His condemnation they procure.

–BROTHER FRANCIS
　PATRICK, F.S.C.

During the course of His ministry, Jesus traveled outside of Galilee a number of times. It was on one such occasion, near Caesarea Philippi, that Jesus asked His disciples, "Who do you say that I am?" (R. Opfer/H. Armstrong Roberts)

PETER AND THE GLORY OF GOD

HENRI DANIEL-ROPS

During the summer of 29, Jesus made a series of journeys outside of Galilee. In June, just after revisiting Jerusalem, He set out for Phoenicia, where it is recorded that He cast out a devil from the daughter of a Canaanite woman. Probably He came back by way of Sidon and crossed the Jordan by the bridge of the Daughters of Jacob, and spent a fortnight or so in one of the towns of the Decapolis. As the heat grew more fierce, He proceeded toward the north among the thickly wooded foothills of Mount Hermon.

Here was the frontier of Palestine, a country where a Jew from Jerusalem, or even Nazareth, would look in vain for familiar things. It was the country of Dan, the northernmost limit of the Promised Land, and after the burning plains of Tiberias it was paradise indeed. The air seemed fresh and cool, and almond trees, fig trees, poplars, and willows grew together in careless profusion.

Jesus and His disciples went among the villages around Caesarea Philippi. Caesarea itself was too infected with paganism for them to visit it. It must have been on one of these terraces looking out at Mount Hermon or on one of those walks where the Jordan foams over the soft sand, so delightful to bare feet, that a scene decisive in the history of the world took place, the formation of the hierarchy of the future Church.

"What do men say of the Son of Man? Who do they think He is?" asked Jesus one day of the Apostles. "Some say John the Baptist, others Elias, others again, Jeremias or one of the prophets. Who do you say that

I am?" He insisted. Simon Peter spoke up: "Thou art the Christ, the Son of the living God." Then Jesus said: "Blessed art thou, Simon son of Jona; it is not flesh and blood; it is My Father in heaven that has revealed this to thee. And I tell thee this in My turn, that thou art Peter, and it is upon this rock that I will build My church; and the gates of hell shall not prevail against it; and I will give thee the keys of the kingdom of heaven; and whatever thou shalt bind on earth shall be bound in heaven; and whatever thou shalt loose on earth shall be loosed in heaven." Then He instructed them to tell no man that He was Christ.

Two fundamental facts are established by the Gospel narrative at this point. The first is the recognition by Peter, in the name of the Twelve, of the divinity of Christ. It was not the first time that the disciples had recognized the nature of their Master. But this formal recognition by Peter had a special significance, coming as it did when the clouds were beginning to gather, when hostility to Jesus was becoming marked and the facile crowds of followers, in spite of the miracles, were falling away. But the Apostles never doubted. They had progressed in faith, and the secret of Christ's mission was about to be entrusted to them, though not now and here where the inimical pagan spirit of the place affronted the Jewish ideal.

They themselves had more to learn before they could understand fully, and that is why Jesus enjoined secrecy upon them and why He was to tell them, a little later, about His coming Passion and Death. They were to become His legatees. The use of the word "Church" immediately afterward has a particular significance. The Christian assembly was to extend the Jewish "community," the *kahal,* in an essential respect. The Church was to participate in the divinity of the Messias, in His glory as in His suffering. ⊛

PETER

Now he walked on the angry
   wave,
Now he sank in the watery
   grave;
Now he rose in triumphant faith,
Now he fell toward threatening
   death,
     Peter, the wave man.

Now he firmly stood for the Lord,
Based his life on the living Word,
Saw in Jesus the Godhead shine,
Dared to call Him the Christ
   divine,
     Peter, the rock man.

Now he rebukes Christ in his pride,
Now he has even his Lord denied;
Now he uses a silly sword,
Now he shrinks at a maiden's word,
     Peter, the wave man.

Now he weeps in his agony;
Now he listens: "Lovest thou Me?"
Now and for aye, as at Pentecost,
He stands for the Saviour that once
   he lost,
     Peter, the rock man.

Rough old fisherman brotherly
   dear,
Near to my weakness, very near,
Far from your folly I would flee,
Brave with your boldness I would be
     Peter, a rock man!

—AMOS RUSSEL WELLS

79

THIS IS MY BELOVED SON

MARJORIE HOLMES

Up and up they climbed, Peter, James, and John, rejoicing, seeing no one except for a few shepherds, grazing their flocks of sheep in the foothills. No preaching and healing today, no crowds to be kept at bay, no sights of human misery, no sounds of wailing and pleading or the horrible hiss that demons sometimes make, spewing from a tortured mouth.

The air was like chilled wine, to be drunk in glorious drafts, making the head light, then even lighter the higher they ascended. They drank it deeply into their lungs, free and young and a trifle giddy, as at a joyous banquet. Peter was soon panting, though beaming as he tried to keep up with James and John.

Jesus was already far ahead. Though he had invited them to go with him, after his first cordial greeting he had set off, with a pace they could not match.

Halfway to the broad white cone, Peter paused to wrap his cloak around him. "Master, wait, we must rest!" he bellowed, shielding his eyes to the glare. But Jesus was too far above them to be seen.

"Do you suppose he's going straight on to the summit?" James, too, was searching the white expanse. "It's a long way and we're tired already, and cold."

"There is something on his mind," they agreed. "Jesus has said almost nothing; he hasn't even looked back."

"Jesus knows we will follow him and find him—wherever he is," Peter said. "It will probably be the highest summit," they decided.

Meanwhile, catching their breath, they gazed in wonder at the magnificent panorama spread before them.

Refreshed, they climbed on, and soon were relieved to

discover the slightly drifted tracks of the one they were following. It was hard going now, the snow deeper, the air even more thin. Everything glistened and sparkled with an intensity Peter had never seen before, even on the water. And it flashed through his mind how his life had changed. From a dull, stolid fisherman, routinely muttering his prayers, seldom attending his synagogue—to this! The very dangers of following Jesus, the terrible possibilities, had added a reckless color and sense of purpose to his life. And to be so close to him—one of the chosen three. Selected to be with Jesus whenever the occasion seemed important. A sudden awareness of that honor struck him afresh.

At last, breathing hard, light-headed, nearly exhausted but filled with anticipation, they reached the place where Jesus

ACCORDING TO SAINT MARK

The way was steep and wild;
    we watched Him go
Through tangled thicket,
    over sharp-edged stone
That tore His feet,
    until He stood alone
Upon the summit where
    four great winds blow;
Fearful we knelt
    on the cold rocks below,
For the o'erhanging cloud
    had larger grown,
A strange still radiance
    through His body shone
Whiter than moonlight
    on the mountain snow.

Then two that flamed
    amber and amethyst
Were either side of Him,
    while low thunder rolled
Down to the ravens
    in their dark ravine;
But when we looked again,
    as through a mist
We saw Him near us.
    —Like a pearl we hold
Close to our hearts
    what we have heard
        and seen.

–THOMAS S. JONES JR.

The Church of the Transfiguration was built atop Mount Tabor, the site many believe was the location of Christ's transfiguration. (R. Kord/H. Armstrong Roberts)

THE TRANSFIGURATION

Few the homages and small
That the guilty earth at all
Was permitted to accord
To her King and hidden Lord.
Dear to us for this account
Is the glory of the Mount,
When bright beams of light
   did spring
Thro' the sackcloth covering.
Rays of glory found their way
Thro' the garment of decay,
With which, as with a cloak, He had
His divinest splendour clad.

–ARCHBISHOP TRENCH

must surely be, and stood blinking and looking about for a moment, their eyes at first half blinded with the sun and snow. Gradually their vision cleared; they saw that it was a broad and level spot, surprisingly covered with green grass, for the sun poured down upon it like a golden funnel. Overhead the sky seemed close enough to touch, a pure cloudless blue. And now they realized they had been led to sacred ground, and even then were witnessing something profound. For at last their eyes began to focus on the one they sought.

And they knew him and knew him not, for he was standing in radiance at the center of the circle, his white garments shimmering beyond even the radiance of the sun-lit snow. Jesus' head was thrown back as if in prayer, his countenance utterly changed—effulgent, transfigured. And awe and terror smote them, so that James and John covered their eyes for an instant and stifled the cries in their throats.

Then they saw, to their further astonishment, that two men were with him. Whence they came and how they got there, the apostles could not fathom. Their eyes sought confirmation from each other, to make sure they were not dreaming. For now, in the stillness, they could hear the men speaking in low tones. And Jesus turned to the strangers and answered them, though it was impossible to hear what was being said. What were they discussing? Could it be perhaps what Jesus was to accomplish in the time he had left? For suddenly they realized—with a shock of recognition it came to Peter, James, and John—these two figures were not of this world.

"Moses! Elijah!" Peter tried to moisten his dry lips. Silently he whispered their names. The prophets had returned, surely with a message straight from heaven.

Peter swayed; he had to fight for control. He must stand fast. He dared not fall prostrate either in awe or in terror, as James and John had done. Why should any miracle overcome him now? After all the miracles he had witnessed! Had he not helped Jesus steady the man climbing down from his bier on his way to the grave? Stood beside Jesus when, with a word and a touch of his hand, he drew life back into a little girl? He needs me, he has made that clear. He has a reason for allowing me to be here with him now. I was the first to acknowledge him as the Christ. He has promised me the keys to heaven!

Oh, to prolong this moment, fix it in time forever, mark it with his zeal! Staggered before the vision, light-headed from the climb, yet he was gripped by sublime conviction, given the courage to step forward. He heard his own voice saying, "Jesus, Master, we are here. We have followed you through the snows to be with you. Now I know why: we must build three tabernacles. Only say the word—one for you, one for Moses, and one for Elijah!"

Even as he spoke, Peter realized, to his dismay, that a bright cloud was coasting over the face of the sun, casting a shadow upon the strangers, so that he could see them less clearly. They were vanishing before his eyes. And as Peter stood frozen in bewilderment, a voice spoke from the cloud in tones both reassuring and yet astounding: "This is my beloved son, with whom I am well pleased. Hear him."

Now Peter, too, hurled himself prostrate upon the ground. In a moment he felt Jesus' hand, warm and firm on his shoulder. "Come, Peter, rise, don't be afraid." One by one Jesus bent over them, touching each in turn. And looking up in awe and wonder, they were relieved to find themselves staring at the same dear familiar face. Jesus was smiling, their friend unchanged. The dazzling white raiment was once more a simple homespun tunic.

"Moses and Elijah have gone," Jesus said simply. "Though they were here. You saw them. It is one reason I wanted you with me. That your faith in the Son of Man might be confirmed. But only to strengthen you for what is to come."

V

THE MIRACLES OF JESUS

And Jesus went about all the

cities and villages, teaching in

their synagogues, and preaching

the gospel of the kingdom, and

healing every sickness and every

disease among the people.

—MATTHEW 9:35

Mine hour is not yet come.

–JOHN 2:4

MIRACLES SUCH AS THE WORLD HAS NEVER SEEN

MARJORIE HOLMES

Here the author fictionalizes a scene between Mary and her mother, Hannah, after the death of Jesus' earthly father, Joseph.

J oseph died that night.

In the shop where he had taught them, Jesus and his brothers hammered and sawed until dawn, building him a bier of finest cedarwood. Toward noon they hoisted their precious burden to their shoulders and carried him, praying aloud, up to the cave in the rocky cleft where the body of Joachim lay.

Jesus, wearing Joseph's prayer shawl, lifted his arms and uttered a prayer of his own composing before the stone was rolled to seal the tomb.

Mary and Hannah supported each other, creeping back down the long hill to the farm. Mary was shivering; the tomb had been damp and chill. She could cry no more. Let people think what they would. The grief that consumed her was too deep for sound; one who will mourn forever cannot expend her strength in screaming.

On the final day of mourning they took off their rough black sackcloth and scrubbed the ashes from their faces. Hannah's cheeks were streaked with blood. She had been caught up in the organized frenzy of grief, after all. She had rent her flesh and her garments and screamed. Now, exhausted, faint with fasting, she was a little ashamed as she remembered Mary's composure all week—bravely trying to comfort her weeping children, and just seeing to all those guests! Such a turnout for Joseph. Never before seen in Nazareth, it pleased her to think. Except, of course, for Joachim . . . *Joachim.* Fresh

(photo, pages 84–85)
Many of Jesus' miracles took place around the Lake of Gennesaret, more commonly known as the Sea of Galilee. It is here that Jesus' disciples observed Him walking on water. (Erich Lessing/Art Resource)

Jesus often used the vine as a metaphor for Himself and His believers as in John 15:5. (Jeanne Conte)

pain struck her, pain so genuine she doubled over with it. Fiercely, Hannah sat hugging herself, as if to crush it from her breast.

"Mother, don't. Please don't." Mary came to stand beside her, to stroke the pitifully balding head.

"But where *are* they?" Hannah moaned, lifting her tiny tormented face. "Joseph and your father?"

"I don't know," Mary said. "But Jesus does."

"Will we ever see them again?"

"Yes. It's what Jesus promised when we stood at the cave."

"How does he know?" Hannah pleaded. She was clutching Mary's hand. "How does he *know?*"

"We must not forget who he is," said Mary. "He is God's son."

"Then why—?" Hannah hesitated, filled with dread. Yet she must speak of it, the question that had taunted her all week. And it came to Hannah that perhaps her screaming, all her screaming, had been only for its answer. "Mary, I can't help wondering," she groped. "I have heard of healings. The holy men, the prophets, sometimes even the rabbis—it may not be true, of course, but I . . . it has been said such men sometimes do miraculous things." Then she blurted it out: "Surely Jesus is greater than any of them. *Why didn't he heal them?*"

Mary closed her eyes, fearing that for the first time she might break. "Nobody loved his father more," she said quietly after a moment. "Or his grandfather either. Oh, Mother, don't you think he would have saved them if he could? But he couldn't, he couldn't, not yet," she moaned softly. "We must be patient, Mother, we must wait. His miracles will come when the One who sent him is ready."

"I may not live to see them," Hannah whispered.

"Yes, you will! And they will be miracles such as the world has never seen."

MIRACLES

Thy miracles in Galilee
When all the world went after Thee
To bless their sick, to touch
    their blind,
O Gracious Healer of Mankind
But fan my faith to brighter glow!
Have I not seen, do I not know
One greater miracle than these?
That Thou, the Lord of Life,
    shouldst please
To walk beside me all the way,
My Comrade of the Everyday.

Was I not blind to beauty, too
Until Thy love came shining through
The dark of self and made me see
I share a glorious world with Thee?
Did I not falter till Thy hand
Reached out to mine? Did I
    not stand
Perplexed and mute and deaf until
I heard Thy gentle "Peace, be still,"
And all the turmoil of my heart
Was silenced and I found my part?

Those other miracles I know
Were far away, were long ago,
But this, that I may see Thy face
Transforming all the commonplace,
May work with Thee, and watch
    Thee bless
My little loaves in tenderness;
This sends me singing on my way,
O Comrade of the Everyday!

—MOLLY ANDERSON HALEY

Now when the sun was setting, all they that had any sick with divers diseases brought them unto Him; and He laid His hands on every one of them, and healed them.

–LUKE 4:40

LO, I AM WITH YOU ALWAYS

Wide fields of corn along the valleys
    spread;
The rain and dews mature the
    swelling vine;
I see the Lord is multiplying bread;
I see Him turning water into wine;
I see Him working all the works
divine
He wrought when Salemward His
    steps were led;
The selfsame miracles around Him
    shine;
He feeds the famished; He revives
    the dead;
He pours the flood of light on
    darkened eyes;
He chases tears, diseases, fiends away;
His throne is raised upon these
    orient skies;
His footstool is the pave whereon
    we pray.
Ah, tell me not of Christ in Paradise,
For He is all around us here today.

–JOHN CHARLES EARLE

OUR LORD

CHARLES DICKENS

Jesus Christ began to cure sick people by only laying His hand upon them; for God had given Him power to heal the sick, and to give sight to the blind, and to do many wonderful and solemn things which are called "the miracles" of Christ. For God had given Jesus Christ the power to do such wonders; and He did them, that people might know He was not a common man, and might believe what He taught them, and also believe that God had sent Him. And many people, hearing this, and hearing that He cured the sick, did begin to believe in Him; and great crowds followed Him in the streets and on the roads wherever He went.

Being followed, wherever He went, by great crowds of people, Jesus went, with His disciples, into a house, to rest. While He was sitting inside, some men brought upon a bed a man who was very ill of what is called the Palsy, so that he trembled all over from head to foot, and could neither stand, nor move. But the crowd being all about the door and windows, and they not being able to get near Jesus Christ, these men climbed up to the roof of the house, which was a low one; and through the tiling at the top, let down the bed, with the sick man upon it, into the room where Jesus sat. When He saw him, Jesus, full of pity, said, "Arise! Take up thy bed, and go to thine own home!" And the man rose up and went away quite well; blessing Him, and thanking God.

Of all the people who came to Him, none were so full of grief and distress as one man who was Ruler or Magistrate over many people; and he wrung his hands, and cried, and said, "O Lord, my daughter—my beautiful, good, innocent little girl, is dead. O come to her, come to her, and lay Thy blessed hand upon her, and I know she will revive, and come

to life again, and make me and her mother happy. O Lord, we love her so, we love her so! And she is dead!"

Jesus Christ went out with him, and so did His disciples, and went to his house, where the friends and neighbors were crying in the room where the poor dead little girl lay, and where there was soft music playing; as there used to be, in those days, when people died. Jesus Christ, looking on her, sorrowfully, said to comfort her poor parents, "She is not dead. She is asleep." Then He commanded the room to be cleared of the people that were in it, and going to the dead child, took her by the hand, and she rose up, quite well, as if she had only been asleep. Oh, what a sight it must have been to see her parents clasp her in their arms, and kiss her, and thank God, and Jesus Christ His son, for such great Mercy!

But He was always merciful and tender. And because Jesus did such Good, and taught people how to love God and how to hope to go to Heaven after death, He was called Our Saviour. ✄

The Roman ruins of Jerash give a glimpse of the beauty of the architecture in Jesus' time. (Jeanne Conte)

> Then those men, when they had seen the miracle that Jesus did, said, This is of a truth that prophet that should come into the world.
>
> –JOHN 6:14

ON THE EVE OF THE FIRST MIRACLE

IVAN NAZHIVIN

The author imagines Jesus in Nazareth, awaiting the moment to take up His mission. He uses the Hebrew names Jeshua and Miriam for Jesus and Mary.

Every time Jeshua came back to visit Galilee, He had a feeling of relief, even of happiness. Here He was surrounded by the wooded hills of His childhood, by the villages with their simple, hardworking population, by luxuriant gardens and vineyards.

Nazareth was then a small quiet town of some three or four thousand inhabitants. Its inhabitants did not disdain either a beaker of wine or a good joke or a merry song, and for that reason the scribes looked down with contempt on this frivolous people: they would say with a sneer—"Can anything good come out of Nazareth?"

His brother Jacob, working at the planing-bench, looked up. "Shelom!" he answered without a smile. He always thought that Jeshua, the eldest of them, abused His position and did too little work. They had hardly exchanged a dozen words when their mother, Miriam, came out from the barn. She was now thin and faded, and her great black eyes were filled with sadness.

A wan smile lit up Miriam's face as she saw her son. She asked Him about His affairs, what He was proposing to do, and how He was. Yet she felt that they had really nothing to say to each other. Jeshua was a fragment that had been broken off; He lived in a world of His own, a world which seemed to the other members of the family to be not only inaccessible but even to some extent hostile.

After the humble meal, eaten in silence in the yard where everyone could see them, Jeshua went up to the roof, anticipating a delicious sleep after such a long journey. A cool and gentle breeze was blowing as it always did in Galilee. The stars shone over His head. In the distant mountains He could hear the howling of jackals.

He fell asleep as the cocks crowed for the third time in the stillness of the night. But hardly had the East begun to redden beyond the mountains when Jeshua was up again, filled with a new readiness for life. And He felt an impulse now to take up the yoke of that peaceful hardworking life which He had led there as a child and which the Galileans around Him were still living. After He had prayed, He came down into the house, turned back His sleeves, tied a string round His hair to prevent it from getting in His way while He was working, and then took up the saw, full of eagerness for work.

And now more frequently than in the past there would come into His mind those passages in the ancient writings which speak of the suffering and death of the one who was to make known the truth. There was particularly the well-known passage in Isaiah, where the prophet speaks—in mysterious words of sadness, which at the same time are filled with the promise of eternal happiness—of the "man of sorrows," the unknown, the despised and persecuted, the man, however, who through His fearlessly borne sufferings would win the right to set up the kingdom of truth and justice. This man is the servant of the eternal, the man who without fear will face destruction in order that He may bring happiness to men.

"Are you coming to Simeon's wedding tomorrow?" His mother asked in a sleepy voice. "You must come."

"I will come," Jeshua answered, tearing Himself away from Isaiah. ▓

THE WEDDING AT CANA

ELIZABETH STUART PHELPS

And the third day there was a
marriage in Cana of Galilee; and
the mother of Jesus was there:
And both Jesus was called, and
His disciples, to the marriage.
And when they wanted wine, the
mother of Jesus saith unto Him,
They have no wine.

Jesus saith unto her, Woman,
what have I to do with thee? Mine
hour is not yet come.

–JOHN 2:1–4

These clay jars may be from the time of
Jesus. Regardless, they are symbolic of His
first miracle at the wedding feast in Cana.
(Jeanne Conte)

It was a Wednesday, the day of the week when Jewish maidens might marry. It was a house of some degree, and all the relatives were there, poor and well-to-do alike.

A group of belated guests, coming up the dusty pathway to the house, attracted [the bride's] giddy and wavering attention. They were six in number, quite ordinary-looking persons, unless one excepted their leader, a young man with a fine mien, who approached the courtyard with the manner of an invited guest, and seemed to expect admission for His five companions. The maiden recognized Him for one of the kinsfolk with whom she did not feel acquainted and wondered why He had not arrived with His mother, who was already among the company.

On a later day of the prolonged festivities, Mary called her son aside and revealed to Him in troubled feminine whispers the great disaster which had befallen the household. What could be worse than for the wine to give out before the entertainment was over? It was no less than a family scandal! She tried to impress it on His mind as such. Jesus looked at her with distant eyes. It seemed a small matter to Him. He listened to His mother deferentially.

Gently putting His mother aside, He said in Aramaic that here was a matter which was not a proper topic of discussion between them.

Then, troubled a little lest He might grieve the tenderest of women—troubled more within Himself as to the nature of His power or of His privilege—half repenting, He offered her His confidence, as much of it as He could, with quick, beautiful, filial trust.

"Mine hour," He whispered, "is not yet come. Leave Me to Myself till Mine hour cometh." Then He remembered that there was a public view of this private, social deed. His new friends stood looking anxiously at Him. His mother, standing in the background, watched Him with luminous, trustful eyes.

Was *this* the time, the place, the sufficient reason, for *that?*—for that strange indwelling, that mystical gift whose scope or depth as yet He could not guess? Would The Source of All Power be troubled with such a matter? Was it Thy Will? . . . Try! Put forth the hand, the heart, the mind, the prayer, the being!

"Fill the water-pots with fresh water. Carry it, and offer it to drink.

"Thou water, that art the source of life, the secret of growth, the food of the blossom and the fruit, the essence of earth and sea and sky, the matrix of creation, thou purer and mightier than the blood of the vine, return upon the steps of law! Omit, be haste, be force, be season, be blossom, be vine, be sap, be grape, be wine! Such is The Will. Obey."

Everybody was talking of the marvel. But He, being overstrained with it, tried to take Himself away. He seemed, indeed, more exhausted than it was easy to explain.

A hubbub set in upon the wedding party. For an hour it seemed quite doubtful whether the young Rabbi were likely to be most popular or most unpopular because of it.

He did not wait to see, but resolutely turned away. His own soul was as much perturbed as elated. So it was true, was real; He could never say to Himself again that those were the hallucinations of a starving brain which mocked Him in the desert. Some one had brought Him a cup and He tremulously put His lips to it. ❈

CANA

Dear Friend! whose presence in
  the house,
Whose gracious word benign,
Could once, at Cana's wedding
  feast,
Change water into wine;

Come, visit us! and when dull
  work
Grows weary, line on line,
Revive our souls, and let us see
Life's water turned to wine.

Gay mirth shall deepen into joy,
Earth's hopes grow half divine,
When Jesus visits us, to make
Life's water glow as wine.

For when self seeking turns to
  love,
Not knowing mine nor thine,
The miracle again is wrought,
And water turned to wine.

—JAMES FREEMAN CLARKE

ONE WHO
CAME TO BRING LIFE

MANUEL KOMROFF

And it came to pass, as He went to Jerusalem, that He passed through the midst of Samaria and Galilee. And as He entered into a certain village, there met Him ten men that were lepers, which stood afar off: And they lifted up their voices, and said, Jesus, Master, have mercy on us.

And when He saw them, He said unto them, Go show yourselves unto the priests. And it came to pass, that, as they went, they were cleansed. And one of them, when he saw that he was healed, turned back, and with a loud voice glorified God, And fell down on his face at His feet, giving Him thanks: and he was a Samaritan.

And Jesus answering said, Were there not ten cleansed? but where are the nine? There are not found that returned to give glory to God, save this stranger. And He said unto him, Arise, go thy way: thy faith hath made thee whole.

–LUKE 17:11–19

In the shadow of a great jagged rock Jesus rested.

A voice which seemed to come from above Him cried out: "Unclean!" It was a cry filled with terror.

He looked up and there, almost directly over Him on top of the great rock, stood an old man in rags.

"Unclean!" he repeated. "Tarry not here. We are outcasts and this valley of rocks belongs to us."

"Praise the Lord in Heaven," Jesus said. "He watches over all men."

"The Lord in Heaven," cried the old man, "has brought this upon us. The one you would have us praise is not here."

"Go!" the old man cried. "What we have here we will share with no one. Go, stranger! We will divide with no one."

"I ask nothing. I am ready to give. How many are you?"

"Four are men; two are women; two are boys; and two are girls. Altogether we are ten."

"You fear not?" the old man asked.

"I fear not. I choose those who suffer. They are My people."

The old man gazed hard at Jesus, then he sank to his knees and bowed his head. "Forgive me," he said. "I did not understand. You come to us as a friend and not as an enemy. Only one thing. Do not ask us to praise the Lord. Would You have us thank Him for our wretchedness?"

Then one of the women spoke up boldly. "He has forsaken us. He has turned a deaf ear to our prayers." And the second woman spoke: "The Lord is an evil Lord."

"There are those," said another, "who live in palaces, and others in huts. Even the oxen are given a shed for the night. But what have we?"

"I bring you life," said Jesus, "and nothing more."

He held out His arms and two of the children ran toward Him. He embraced them and stroked their heads. Suddenly they burst into tears.

"Tell Me why you are weeping," He asked.

"I do not know," said one.

But the other looked into His face and said: "A strange feeling, almost frightening, came over me. And in my head, before my eyes, the heavens seemed to open. And Your words were true. He who sits on the throne in heaven watches over everyone. Even we who are poor and sick and have nothing: He loves even us. And I will pray to Him."

"He loves you all," Jesus said. "And you who are poor and sick and have nothing: you are no longer poor and no longer sick, and the world that belongs to all people now also belongs to you. Go, show yourselves unto the priests, and let them see that you have been cleansed."

All who were standing now sank to their knees and held their white arms up toward heaven. And slowly, very slowly, the red of life returned to their limbs until it had reached their fingertips.

The outcasts lost no time. One by one they rose and walked away silently between the great rocks of the wilderness. But the old man, the one who had stood over Jesus on the great rock and waved his staff in the air, fell down at His feet.

"Forgive me," he pleaded. "I have done more than the others. It was I who forbade You to tarry. It was I who threatened You. And it was I who gathered the other nine to frighten You away. Envy and hate were in my heart. Forgive me."

"You are forgiven. But will you forget that one passed here by chance? I have come to bring you life. Go. Hurry. Join the others and live once more. Forget or remember, it matters little. Only one thing matters. Believe and have faith."

CHRIST, THE GOOD PHYSICIAN

Jesus, Thy far-extended fame
My drooping soul exults to hear;
Thy name, Thy all-restoring name,
Is music in a sinner's ear.

Sinners of old Thou didst receive
With comfortable words, and kind;
Their sorrows cheer, their wants
    relieve,
Heal the diseased, and cure the blind.

And art Thou not the Saviour still,
In every place and age the same?
Hast Thou forgot Thy gracious
    skill,
Or lost the virtue of Thy name?

Faith in Thy changeless name I
    have.
The good, the kind Physician,
    Thou
Art able now our souls to save,
Art willing to restore them now.

—CHARLES WESLEY

JESUS FEEDS THE MULTITUDE

GRACE NOLL CROWELL

The day wore on and evening came. Jesus was weary after the strenuous day, and He knew the others were extremely tired. He turned to Philip, the one who stood nearest Him, and asked, "Whence shall we buy bread, that these may eat?"

Andrew was standing by and said, "There is a lad here, which hath five barley loaves, and two small fishes: but what are they among so many?"

Let us go back to the morning and to this boy with the basket. His name may have been Jonas. One may well believe that back at his home he had been pruning the grapevines in his father's vineyard, and that he had looked up suddenly, and had seen in the distance a great crowd hurrying by.

No doubt he ran into the house to find his mother, calling her attention to the throng and begging her to let him go with them. He was sure that the Miracle Worker, of whom he had heard so much, was the one walking a bit ahead of the others, and he longed mightily to see that man.

At first his mother may have objected, telling him that he was too young to go, that the way would be too long, as is the way with mothers; but when she saw his disappointment and noticed the tears gathering in his eyes, she decided it really could do no harm for him to go with the rest that beautiful summer morning, and perhaps he could get to see the strange man of whom they had heard so much. That would be good, she thought.

She turned hastily, gathering up a basket and placing in it a few barley biscuits and a couple of fish left from the morning meal. She told him he would have to hurry or he

would be left behind. And hurry he did. He came to the edge of the crowd and found another lad of his own age who seemingly was very weary. He was lame, and Jonas put his shoulder under the boy's arm; the crutch helped the other side, and they hastened to catch up with the others.

Jonas listened intently. The words borne on the air were like nothing he had ever heard before: they were words of tenderness and love, gentle words that touched the boy to sudden tears. The man Himself drew him as a magnet draws steel. Soon the crowd was pressing forward—

These rock steps lead from the Church of Tabgah into the Sea of Galilee. This is thought to be the site of the miracle of the multiplication of the fishes and loaves. (Erich Lessing/Art Resource)

97

closer—closer—Jonas and his companion were perforce pushed nearer the speaker.

They watched Him touch blind eyes and sight was restored. They saw the lame leap for joy after this One had said the freeing word. They heard the loud rejoicing of the dumb, freed at last from their lifetime bondage.

Jonas took his companion by the arm and drew him nearer the Healer. He said excitedly: "You, too, can be healed. You can run and jump as I can. Come, let Him touch you." And sure enough, the gentle hands reached out to the young lad and healing came. And oh, the joy of it! Jonas had never seen anyone as happy as his newly found friend. To see one who lifelong had been hurt, freed from that hurt, was a blessed experience.

The sun was setting now, and Jonas heard himself being singled out by the man Andrew. He had turned perplexed eyes on the throng. There were thousands needing to be fed. He had spied Jonas and his small basket. "Here, lad, may I take your basket?" he asked. Eagerly the lad handed over the basket, food and all, for he had forgotten to eat his lunch, so engrossed had he become in the man who had been speaking. Andrew handed the basket to the Master, half reluctantly. What would these small loaves and few fishes be among so many!

"Make them sit down," Jesus commanded, and down they sat on the clean, sweet-smelling grass and waited His further orders. After the giving of thanks, the man opened the basket, and behold! Loaf after loaf, fish after fish came forth, until Jonas, his eyes all but popping out of his head, could scarcely believe what he saw.

Even after all hunger had been satisfied, other baskets appeared from nowhere, until twelve of them were filled with fragments that were left. Jesus impressed upon the crowd that waste was sinful, and to this day His words bear lasting fruit to those who live by His word.

Jonas heard the voices about him speaking with wonder: "Here is of truth a prophet that shall come into the world." The boy did not doubt that statement. As he and his companion turned homeward they scarcely could contain themselves, so great was their exultation and delight. Jonas said: "I shall keep my basket always, and I shall remember the miracle wrought through it." And his companion leaped and skipped, trying his new-found legs with joy.

"Was ever anyone so kind before?" cried Jonas. "Was there anyone who cared so greatly for the people? I shall go telling of this day and of that man who can do all things. I shall call out to everyone to come see that man." ▧

BARLEY BREAD

As I was going down the street
    to sell my loaves of barley,
A crowd of men were following
    the man from Nazareth,
And I in wonder followed too,
Outside the town where lilies grew,
And cyclamen, and bells of blue—
I ran till out of breath.

"Barley bread, barley bread!
    Who will buy my barley?
Sweet and crisp as any
    from the oven in the square,
Buy my loaves of bread, and fish
Freshly caught as one could wish"—
I followed them beyond the town
    and found Him waiting there.

They came with jingling silver then
    and bought my bread and fishes;
He broke them there in sight of all
    and lifted up His hands.
And everyone had food to eat—
My fish as good as any meat,
And barley bread, so brown and sweet,
Enough for His demands.

O Teacher out of Nazareth,
    if I have aught to give You,
Take, take the little that I have,
    just as You took my food,
For till today I never heard
A thing so moving as Your word;
So take my loaves of barley bread
    and feed the multitude.

—HILDA W. SMITH

Even the
Winds and Sea Obey

Marjorie Holmes

And when He was entered into a ship, His disciples followed Him. And, behold, there arose a great tempest in the sea, insomuch that the ship was covered with the waves: but He was asleep. And His disciples came to Him, and awoke Him, saying, Lord, save us: we perish.

—MATTHEW 8:23–25

The storm struck swiftly. Peter, steering the ship in a diagonal course across the lake, was not at first concerned. But a blast of wind nearly tore the rudder from his hands, and he began to bark orders.

James and John were already darting about like monkeys; the other men, drowsing below or on the deck, threw off their cloaks and came running to help. Even Judas, who knew little of wind and canvas, sprang to the task, obediently following commands.

Where is Jesus? Peter worried. James had reported that he was sleeping. How could anyone lie peacefully sleeping, as if this were a night of calm seas?

Judas, drenched to the skin and terrified now, was suddenly at Peter's elbow. "Where is our Master? Why isn't he up here with us?"

"Say no word against him!" Peter bellowed. Yet his own fear had begun to poison his heart. What am I doing following this man who has promised us the kingdom, yet lies sleeping while the waves are like whales threatening to devour us?

A glassy mountain, huge, dark, glistening, was suddenly upon them, bashing the boat. At the same instant there was another flash of lightning. Half blinded by the light, stunned by a blow on his head, Peter found himself on his hands and knees. "I will go fetch him," he panted. "He will save us."

Peter began fighting his way toward Jesus, Andrew and Philip just behind him. Another flash of light revealed the still white form, the curly head propped peacefully against the wooden pillow. So utterly still. "Master, wake up, wake up!" he screamed.

Jesus sat up, blinking, and gazed at them, for an instant bewildered. Then he, too, felt the pitching and rolling, heard the furies. Springing to his feet, he pushed past them and strode to the rail.

They saw him standing there for a moment, feet apart, bracing himself with his hands. His head was back, his chin out-thrust, his face lifted to the storm, as if to welcome its cold wet torrents and the wind that so wildly blew his hair. There was power and dignity in his stance, as if he were embracing its very assault. He lifted his arms in a gesture of both authority and release. "Peace, be still!" he cried out.

Fishermen today still cast their nets into the Sea of Galilee as did Jesus' disciples so many years ago. (Jeanne Conte)

The men could feel the boat shuddering under their feet. They staggered and clung to each other as it gave a final lurch. Looking up in amazement, they realized the avalanche of rain had stopped. Only a few scattered drops still fell. The wind had ceased. The angry sea calmed; the very skies began to clear until only a few clouds remained, scudding across the face of a placid moon.

Jesus turned and beckoned to them. "It grieves me that you were so troubled," he said kindly. "Have you not yet learned there is nothing to fear so long as you are with me? Why does it take you so long to believe in the Father who sent me? Where is your faith?"

Awed, they went back to mop up the deck, repair the battered sails. The night was far gone. They discussed it among themselves until morning, marveling at this man who could not only heal the sick and raise the dead but command the storm. Who was he that even the winds and the raging seas obeyed him? ✠

HEALING ON THE SABBATH

ELIZABETH STUART PHELPS

Now there is at Jerusalem by the sheep market a pool, which is called in the Hebrew tongue Bethesda, having five porches. In these lay a great multitude of impotent folk, of blind, halt, withered, waiting for the moving of the water.

–JOHN 5:2–3

Jesus stood beside Bethesda, and it was the Sabbath—the awful Sabbath, in which a man was forbidden to carry fuel, a rug, a bundle, or to lift the sick upon their beds. Only the dying could be carried by good Jews. A medical cure was forbidden. Jesus stood watching the mass of misery that had accumulated at the pool. His now practiced eye perceived among those wretched people a large proportion of nervous patients, and among them He readily recognized the worst and most genuine case. A helpless man, disabled for thirty-eight years, and deserted by his friends who had grown tired of taking care of him, lay sadly in one of the porches by himself. This was the sickest man at the spring, and the only one sure to receive no attention.

Jesus went directly to him. The two were apart. No one noticed the Rabbi who came to see Bethesda, a common resort for country folk visiting Jerusalem and anxious to see the sights. Jesus entered at once into conversation with the disabled man, who had attracted His interest. He did not insult the nervous patient by expressing doubts as to the reality of his disorder. He did not prejudge hysterical symptoms or underestimate the nature of a suffering only too evident to His refined perception. An ordinary physician might easily have turned this case off as one of the Bethesda hypochondriacs.

The Galilean healer was too sensitive for that. His mind was too keen to make this blunder, because it was too fine. Gently drawing from the poor man his story, which was not altogether that of an innocent sufferer, He sorrowed for the patient more than He blamed. His heart ached at the plaintive and uncomplaining, "Sir, all the others can get into the water, but there is nobody to help me. Before I can get down—"

But there the stranger interrupted him. The morbid, motionless man clinging to his superstition because he had nothing better, looked, startled, up. What words were these? What face was that? What fire, half of indignation, half of pity, played across those gentle features? Why did the Rabbi shake His head?

What? Not believe in the waters—not in the *Bethesda* waters—after all? Believe only in this face, this voice, this sweetest sympathy ever found in all a lonely, miserable life? With a rush of emotion, it suddenly seemed to the neglected invalid that if he had been dead he could have lived had this man spoken to him, had he looked at Him so.

"Take it up!" cried the stranger, pointing to the bed. "Carry it. Walk!"

With this authoritative order, He dismissed the case and took Himself hurriedly away.

Later in the day Jesus met His cured patient accidentally and exchanged with him a few words. But these were not many, for the story was now public property, and a curious crowd crushed upon the two.

A sullen excitement had set in over the case. Both had defied the law; the healer had wrought a cure, and the invalid had carried a bed upon the Sabbath day.

Ecclesiastical feeling ran high. A timid man would have retreated from it. Jesus, on the contrary, went straight to the Temple, where He was sure to meet the full brunt of it. His object in coming to Jerusalem at that time had been no light one. He was no mere traveler, no comfortable worshiper.

The character of His own peculiar mission asked Him awful questions. These gave Him no rest. He came, and He came alone, definitely to test the attitude of the capital towards Himself. His method of doing this was entirely His own.

In the cause of humanity He had boldly broken the

The ruins of the Pool of Bethesda, where Jesus healed a crippled man, were only recently unearthed. They lie within the walls of the Old City of Jerusalem.
(Jeanne Conte)

Sabbath laws, ancient as Moses, precious as Israel, rigid as death. In the cause of common sense He had treated a superstition dear to Jerusalem with unpardonable contempt. Could He not have cured His man on any other of six days out of seven? Could He not have done it at some time when the spring *did* rise? All ecclesiastical laws and pathological precedents He had simply ignored. The clergy, the people, and the government were equally offended. Not fully prepared for the consequences, Jesus calmly awaited them. If He felt any agitation, He did not show it. In the Temple He serenely defended Himself. A mob was the result.

The very madness of joy looked at Him from the eyes of one adoring man—the escaped prisoner of thirty-eight years of misery. He could see His Bethesda patient excitedly arguing the case with scribe and priest and Pharisee. But the church frowned on the heretic. The people imitated the church. His own discourse in the Temple, a powerful and fearless address, had made everything worse. The country Rabbi became in an hour dangerously unpopular. With hurt surprise, with pathetic wonder that left no room for fear, Jesus perceived that He stood in the Temple of His race, in the holy city of His heart, in actual peril of His life.

His independence of conviction soon brought more trouble upon Him. Having heartily allowed His hungry disciples to pick corn on the Seventh Day, He found that He had committed an unpardonable offense. Jesus defended His innovation warmly and authoritatively. "I am Lord of the Sabbath," He said.

BETHESDA

I saw again the spirits on a day,
Where on the earth in mournful case they lay;
Five porches were there, and a pool and round,
Huddling in blankets, strewn upon the ground,
Tied-up and bandaged, weary, sore, and spent,
The maimed and halt, diseased and impotent.
For a great angel came, 'twas said, and stirred
The pool at certain seasons, and the word
Was, with this people of the sick, that they
Who in the waters here their limbs should lay
Before the motion of the surface ceased
Should of their torment straightway be released.
So with shrunk bodies and with heads down-dropt,
Stretched on the steps, and at the pillars propt,
Watching by day and listening through the night,
They filled the place, a miserable sight.

But what the waters of that pool might be,
Of Lethe were they, or Philosophy;
And whether he, long waiting, did attain
Deliverance from the burden of his pain
There with the rest; or whether, yet before
Some more diviner stranger passed the door
With His small company into that sad place,
And breathing hope into the sick man's face,
Bade him take up his bed, and rise and go.

–A. H. CLOUGH

JESUS RAISES LAZARUS

ELIZABETH GOUDGE

And when He thus had spoken,
He cried with a loud voice,
Lazarus, come forth. Then many
of the Jews which came to Mary,
and had seen the things which
Jesus did, believed on Him.

–JOHN 11:43, 45

LAZARUS

When Lazarus left his charnel-cave,
And home to Mary's house returned,
Was this demanded—if he yearned
To hear her weeping by his grave?

"Where wert thou, brother, these
    four days?"
There lives no record of reply,
Which telling what it is to die
Had surely added praise to praise.

From every house the neighbours
    met,
The streets were filled with joyful
    sound
A solemn gladness even crowned
The purple brows of Olivet.

Behold a man raised up by Christ!
The rest remaineth unrevealed;
He told it not; or something sealed
The lips of that Evangelist.

–ALFRED, LORD TENNYSON

The winter passed and the spring came again, with green shoots on the vines and the voices of the birds, and a message was brought to Our Lord from Martha and Mary to tell Him that Lazarus was ill. "Lord, behold, he whom Thou lovest is sick."

"This sickness is not unto death," Our Lord told His disciples, "but for the glory of God, that the Son of God might be glorified thereby." For two days He stayed where He was in the Jordan Valley, and then He said to His disciples, "Our friend Lazarus sleepeth; but I go, that I may awake him out of sleep."

Lazarus had been dead for four days when Our Lord reached Bethany. Martha and Mary were in their house, and many friends from Jerusalem were with them, trying to comfort them, when they heard that He was coming along the road beyond the village. Mary was too stricken to leave the house, but Martha got up at once and went to meet Him.

"Lord, if Thou hadst been here, my brother had not died," she cried out in her grief when she reached Him.

"I am the resurrection, and the life: he that believeth in Me, though he were dead, yet shall he live: And whosoever liveth and believeth in Me shall never die."

Our Lord honored all women, forever, by speaking these words to a woman; Martha affirmed the faith of all Christian women in every age when to Our Lord's question, "Believest thou this?" she answered, "Yea, Lord: I believe that Thou art the Christ, the Son of God, which should come into the world."

"Where have ye laid him?" He asked, and they answered, "Lord, come and see," and brought Him to the cave in the hillside where they had laid the body, the mouth of the cave closed by a great stone.

Surrounded by the wailing people, facing that closed grave, Our Lord wept. He wept for the sorrow of Mary and Martha, and in this moment He bore also the weight of the grief of the world and wept for the grief of every one of us when we suffer in parting from those we love.

"Take ye away the stone," He commanded.

There was a moment of horrified silence, and then in a silence full of awe and fear the men who were there moved forward, leaned their weight against the stone, and slowly rolled it away. While they did this Our Lord was silently praying to His Father, praying that His great will might be done, praying for Himself and for Lazarus that they might have the strength to perform it, to do this hard thing and obey.

"Father, I thank Thee that Thou hast heard Me. And I knew that Thou hearest Me always: but because of the people which stand by I said it, that they may believe that Thou has sent Me." And then He cried with a loud voice, "Lazarus, come forth."

And Lazarus came out of the dark tomb into the sunlight, but still bound about with the grave clothes and with a napkin about his head and face so that he could not see it.

"Loose him, and let him go," cried Our Lord, and there seems to be almost a note of anguish in His voice, as though He felt with Lazarus the hard pressure of those tightly wound grave clothes, pressing upon what must have seemed in these first moments of return the intolerable prison of the body.

The story stops there abruptly, and not even in imagination can we dare to be with Our Lord and Lazarus in the days that followed. ✹

Lazarus's tomb lies on the southeastern slopes of the Mount of Olives, not far from the home of Lazarus, Mary, and Martha in Bethany. The entrance, a bare, broken hole in an ancient wall, leads down twenty-two steps to the cave of Lazarus's tomb. (Jeanne Conte)

VI

THE PROPHECY FULFILLED

And they were in the way going up to

Jerusalem; and Jesus went before them: and they

were amazed; and as they followed, they were

afraid. And He took again the twelve, and began

to tell them what things should happen unto

Him, Saying, Behold, we go up to Jerusalem;

and the Son of man shall be delivered unto the

chief priests, and unto the scribes; and they shall

condemn Him to death, and shall deliver Him

to the Gentiles. —MARK 10:32–33

THE ENTRY INTO JERUSALEM

CANON FARRAR

On the next day much people that were come to the feast, when they heard that Jesus was coming to Jerusalem, Took branches of palm trees, and went forth to meet Him, and cried, Hosanna: Blessed is the King of Israel that cometh in the name of the Lord.

—JOHN 12:12–13

The Golden Gate is believed to be the gate through which Jesus entered Jerusalem on Palm Sunday. It is now sealed, as it has been for centuries. (Jeanne Conte)

It was no seditious movement to stir up political enthusiasm, no "insulting vanity" to commemorate ambitious triumph. Nay, it was a mere outburst of provincial joy, the simple exultation of poor Galileans and despised disciples. Jesus mounted the unused foal, and no sooner had He started than the multitude spread out their upper garments to tapestry His path, and kept tearing or cutting down the boughs of olive and fig and walnut to scatter them before Him. Then, in a burst of enthusiasm, the disciples broke into the shout, "Hosanna to the Son of David! Blessed is the King of Israel that cometh in the name of the Lord! Hosanna in the highest!" and the multitude caught up the joyous strain and told each other how He had raised Lazarus from the dead.

The road slopes by a gradual ascent up the Mount of Olives, through green fields and under shady trees, till it suddenly sweeps round to the northward. It is at this angle of the road that Jerusalem, which hitherto has been hidden by the shoulder of the hill, bursts full upon the view. As He gazed on that "mass of gold and snow," was there no pride, no exultation in the heart of its true King? Far from it! He had dropped silent tears at the grave of Lazarus; here He wept aloud.

There had been a pause in the procession while Jesus shed His bitter tears and uttered His prophetic lamentation. But now the people in the valley of Kidron, and about the walls of Jerusalem, and the pilgrims whose booths and tents stood so thickly on the green slopes below, had caught sight of the approaching company, and heard the echo of the glad shouts, and knew what the commotion meant. At that time the palms were numerous in the neighborhood of Jerusalem, though now but a few remain: and tearing down their green and graceful branches, the people streamed up the road to meet the approaching Prophet.

Mingled among the crowd were some of the Pharisees, and the joy of the multitude was to them gall and wormwood. What meant these Messianic cries and kingly titles? Were they not dangerous and unseemly? Why did He allow them? "Master, rebuke Thy disciples." But He would not do so. "If these should hold their peace," He said, "the stones would immediately cry out." The words may have recalled to them the threats which occur, amid denunciations against covetousness and cruelty, and the utter destruction by which they should be avenged, in the prophet Habakkuk. The Pharisees felt that they were powerless to stay the flood of enthusiasm.

And when they reached the walls, the whole city was stirred with powerful excitement and alarm. "Who is this?" they asked as they leaned out of the lattices and from the roofs and stood aside in the bazaars and streets to let them pass; and the multitude answered, with something of pride in their great countryman, but already, as it were, with a shadow of distrust falling over their high Messianic hopes: "This is Jesus, the Prophet of Nazareth."

Before they had reached the Shushan gate of the Temple they dispersed, and Jesus entered. The Lord whom they sought had come suddenly to His Temple, even the messenger of the covenant; but they neither recognized Him, nor delighted in Him.

PALM SUNDAY

Come, drop your branches, strew
    the way,
Plants of the day!
Whom sufferings make most green
    and gay.
The King of grief, the man of sorrow
weeping still, like the wet morrow,
Your shades and freshness comes
    to borrow.

Trees, flowers, and herbs; birds,
    beasts, and stones,
That since man fell, expect with
    groans
To see the Lamb, come, all at once,
Lift up your heads and leave
    your moans!
For here comes He
Whose death will be
Man's life, and your full liberty.

Hark! how the children shrill and
    high
"Hosanna" cry;
Their joys provoke the distant sky,
Where thrones and seraphims reply;
And their own angels shine and sing
In a bright ring:
Such young, sweet mirth
Makes heaven and earth
Join in a joyful symphony.

—HENRY VAUGHAN

(photo, pages 108–109)
Jesus likely walked this road from Jericho to Jerusalem; it was built in the era of Emperor Hadrian. (Erich Lessing/Art Resource)

THE HOUSE OF PRAYER

Thy mansion is the Christian's
    heart,
O Lord, thy dwelling-place
    secure!
Bid the unruly throng depart,
And leave the consecrated door.

Devoted as it is to Thee,
A thievish swarm frequents the
    place;
They steal away my joys from me,
And rob my Savior of His praise.

I know them, and I hate their
    din,
Am weary of the bustling crowd;
But while their voice is heard
    within,
I cannot serve Thee as I would.

Oh! for the joy Thy presence
    gives,
What peace shall reign
    when Thou art here!
Thy presence makes
    this den of thieves
A calm, delightful house of
    prayer.

And if Thou make Thy Temple
    shine,
Yet, self-abased, will I adore;
The gold and silver are not mine,
I give Thee what was Thine
    before.

—WILLIAM COWPER

THE CLEANSING OF THE TEMPLE

NORMAN VINCENT PEALE

Well, this day, I followed Jesus and the disciples into the Temple area. The ceilings are adorned with sculptured panels of cedar wood. I've heard it said they are the most beautiful in the world.

But what goes on in this holy place is not beautiful. The air is filled with the cries of penned-up cattle, goats, sheep, pigeons, and doves awaiting slaughter. The stench of blood is sickening. Why should God's dumb creatures be killed this way? the people wonder. How can such sacrifices take away your sin? The God whom Jesus talked about asks for no such sacrifices.

But the people who sell these animals to the worshiper receive a good fee, and old Annas and Caiaphas, the ungodly high priests who run the system, receive a profit. They have still another business. They won't allow Roman money to be used in the Temple or for the purchase of sacrificial animals. This "tainted" money of the conqueror has to be changed into Jewish money. There are many tables and booths set up for the money-changers. It is known that these men make a profit, a big share of which is also added to the ill-gotten riches of Annas and his crowd.

Even that isn't the worst of it. A practice of discrimination has developed. The religion of the prophets teaches regard for the stranger and for people of other races. The great prophet Isaiah called the Temple "a house of prayer for all nations." Yet a large sign in Greek letters was put up at the entrance of the inner court, reading: "Let no foreigner enter within the screen and enclosure around the Holy

Place. Whosoever is taken so doing will himself be the cause that death overtakes him."

On this day, as Jesus stood beneath the sign, I could sense His displeasure. He preached about a God of love; that all men are brothers and that real religion is of the mind and heart.

Suddenly, He blazed with anger. It was a powerful, terrifying anger. Reaching down, He picked up some strands of cord and quickly braided them into a rope. Then, brandishing the rope above His head, He cried in a voice that boomed like thunder, "Take these things away."

With unbridled fury, He overturned the money-changers' tables. Clinking coins rolled in every direction. He jerked open the pens and cages, and soon the area was filled with milling animals and fluttering birds. It was wonderful.

The dealers were stunned. One man started scooping up the money. Another approached as if to oppose Him, but one look into the eyes of Jesus and the man changed his mind.

Clear as a bell, Jesus' scornful words rang out: "You shall not make My Father's house a house of trade." As the last of the dealers, followed by the priests, ran from His fury, He tore down that sign of discrimination, crying out so all could hear: "Is it not written, 'My house shall be called a house of prayer for all the nations?'"

A strange silence fell. Then, beginning slowly, a few cheers started, followed by a deep, surging roar of approval. The exploited people had a champion at last. ▓

And the blind and the lame came to Him in the Temple; and He healed them. And when the chief priests and scribes saw the wonderful things that He did, and the children crying in the Temple, and saying, Hosanna to the son of David; they were sore displeased.

—MATTHEW 21:14–15

Chorazim is one of the cities reprimanded by Jesus for not repenting; below are ruins of the village and its synagogue. (Erich Lessing/Art Resource)

THE LAST SUPPER

NORMAN VINCENT PEALE

And wheresoever he shall go in, say ye to the goodman of the house, The Master saith, Where is the guest-chamber, where I shall eat the passover with My disciples? And he will show you a large upper room furnished and prepared: there make ready for us.

And His disciples went forth, and came into the city, and found as He had said unto them: and they made ready the passover. And in the evening He cometh with the twelve.

–MARK 14:14–17

On Thursday evening, Jesus told His disciples to prepare the Passover supper. It was held in an upper room provided by a man who loved Jesus. Of course, I was not present at the supper: It was only for the twelve, but afterward, I talked with the various apostles, particularly with my father [Andrew] and with the disciples Matthew, Peter, John, and Mark. From the slightly different story each related, I am able to tell you what went on during that final meeting of the Teacher with His friends.

It seems that when all had gathered in the upper room and were about to sit at table, the old argument arose as to who was the favored man in the group. Jesus was saddened by this display of vanity. He reminded His disciples again that in His spiritual kingdom, the great man is the one who serves the most and with the most humble spirit. Such a man would not seek to be saluted and given the best seat but would always try to put others first and always think of Christ's cause more than of himself. Jesus took a basin and towel and went around the room washing the feet of the disciples to show them that even He, their Teacher, was not too proud to perform a humble service. This shamed them, and they quickly took places at the table. As it turned out, John sat at the Master's right—and Judas at His left.

After they were seated, Jesus looked at His disciples, letting His gaze rest lovingly upon each one. These were His close friends and comrades. With them, He had walked the roadways of Judea and Galilee. He had talked with them under the stars. They had been with Him in high moments and in hours of pain. For all their weaknesses and faults, He loved them dearly. But now the days of earthly fellowship

This room on Mount Zion, just outside the walls of Old Jerusalem, commemorates the room in which the Last Supper was held. (Jeanne Conte)

He riseth from supper, and laid aside His garments; and took a towel, and girded Himself. After that He poureth water into a basin, and began to wash the disciples' feet, and to wipe them with the towel wherewith He was girded. Then cometh He to Simon Peter: and Peter saith unto Him, Lord, dost Thou wash my feet? Jesus answered and said unto him, What I do thou knowest not now; but thou shalt know hereafter. Peter saith unto Him, Thou shalt never wash my feet. Jesus answered him, If I wash thee not, thou hast no part with Me. Simon Peter saith unto Him, Lord, not my feet only, but also my hands and my head.

–JOHN 13:4–9

were over. He must go away, and they would have to take charge. He hoped they were ready. He told them how much He wanted to have these last hours of companionship with them. My father said it was very touching to hear Him talk, and they realized how very much they loved Him.

Then, in a voice of great sorrow, He said, "One of you will betray Me."

The disciples could not believe their ears. They all began to talk at once. Strangely enough, they did not accuse each other, but each man asked, "Is it I, Lord?" That any one of them would actually betray Him to the Pharisees never entered their minds. They thought He meant betrayal of His teachings.

He raised His hand to silence them. John told me that Jesus then said, "It is he to whom I shall give this morsel when I have dipped it." They watched, fascinated, as He dipped a morsel of bread in the dish and handed it to Judas Iscariot.

But still the disciples had no idea of how terrible the betrayal would be. Only Jesus and Judas were aware of the hidden meaning of this conversation.

Then, Jesus spoke softly to Judas alone, "What you are going to do, do quickly." Judas looked at him stricken, his face flushed. He rose from the table and went out. The remaining disciples assumed Judas had gone on some errand for the Master. But they were soon to discover that his leaving was a prelude to tragedy.

Jesus then stood up and, taking a loaf of unleavened bread, He blessed it and broke it and gave the pieces to His disciples, saying, "Take, eat; this is My body." He poured out a cup of wine, blessed it, and said, "Drink of it, all of you, for this is My blood of the covenant, which is poured out for many for the forgiveness of sins."

After the disciples had done as He requested, the air of sadness was dispelled. The Master began to talk with tender quality and spirit. His words were aglow with wonder and glory. He was telling His friends that He was going away; that they could not go with Him but would follow.

"Let not your hearts be troubled," He said. "In My Father's house are many rooms. I go to prepare a place for you. I will come again and take you to Myself, that where I am you may be also."

I was charmed by these words when John repeated them to me, and I asked their meaning. John explained that while we, like the Master, would die, Jesus would come for us after death and take us to a beautiful place, there to be with Him always.

John said, and the others also, that Jesus kept stressing that the disciples should love one another. He reminded them that it was His mission to change the world through love, not by force, and that only as the disciples practiced love among themselves could we hope to improve the world. He pointed out that the greatest form of love is to lay down your life for your friend. He even told them that if they continued to believe and love, they would actually do greater things in the future than He had done. That, of course, is hard to imagine, but it is what He said, and it must be so.

John said that an inspiring moment occurred as the disciples were about to part as an earthly band. Jesus prayed for them. He thanked God for giving these men to Him and for their belief in Him as the Son of God. He asked God to watch over them, now that He was leaving. Earnestly, He prayed that they would maintain the spirit of love and unity that existed among them. He told God that He had lost only one. He did not ask an easy path for the others, only that each one might keep the faith. Then, Jesus prayed for all the other disciples too, that each might so live that the world would believe.

THE LAST SUPPER

We give You thanks, holy Father,
for Your holy name,
which You planted in our hearts;
and for the knowledge, faith,
    and immortality
which You sent us through
    Jesus Christ, Your child.

Glory to You throughout the ages.

You created everything,
    sovereign Lord,
for the glory of Your name.
You gave food and drink to men
for their enjoyment,
and as a cause for thanksgiving.
And to us You have given
spiritual food and spiritual drink,
bestowing on us the promise of
    eternal life.
Above all we thank You
for the power of Your love.

Glory to You throughout the ages.

—THE DIDACHE

IN THE GARDEN

JIM BISHOP

Verily I say unto you, I will drink no more of the fruit of the vine, until that day that I drink it new in the kingdom of God. And when they had sung an hymn, they went out into the mount of Olives.

—MARK 14:25–26

JESUS PRAYS ALONE

'Tis midnight; and on Olive's brow
The star is dimmed that lately
    shone:
'Tis midnight; in the garden, now,
The suffering Saviour prays alone.

'Tis midnight; and for others' guilt
The Man of Sorrows weeps in
    blood;
Yet He that hath in anguish knelt
Is not forsaken by His God.

'Tis midnight; and from ether
    plains
Is borne the song that angels know;
Unheard by mortals are the strains
That sweetly soothe the Saviour's
    woe.

—WILLIAM B. TAPPAN

The work was finished. There was an end to the preaching; an end to the miracles; an end to the instruction of the apostles; and even an end to prophecy.

It was a time for waiting. Jesus motioned to Peter and James and John. These three, in whom He reposed special trust, followed Him into the shadows of a little olive garden. He stopped under the trees. In the pattern of the foliage which blotted part of the moonlight, they saw the face of Jesus, and it held fear and horror. As a man He was able to sustain the fullness of suffering; as the man of God He had a knowledge of what was to come.

To the apostles, He seemed to be immeasurably weary. They fell mute and turned their eyes away because they did not think that it was right to look upon the face of the Messiah in weakness and fear.

He doubled his hands into fists and held them against His breast. "Stay here and keep awake," He said with entreaty.

They nodded in silence and watched Him make His way through the low-branched trees for a short distance. There, He paused beside a big flat rock, knelt for a few moments; then, abandoning Himself to overwhelming mortal fear, threw himself full length on the rock, face down. In a loud voice He said: "My Father, if it is possible, let this cup be spared Me!" The lament came, almost involuntarily, from the lips. "And yet," He said, as though afraid to be afraid, "not as I will, but as You will."

No one knew better than Jesus that if He died as the Son of God the gesture would be small, the sacrifice negligible. From this moment until the hour when He expired He knew that He would have to suffer much more than anyone else who might travel the same path and endure the same things; the mere waiting was almost beyond Him. Every minute of every hour must now be borne as a man with extraordinary courage in order to achieve the victory of the one God.

The three who reclined against olive trees in the garden fell asleep, as had the eight on the other side of the road. Thus in the little grove was the incongruous sound of the Son of Man beseeching mercy and, mingled with it, the sleep-borne noises of healthy men whose faculties had been short-circuited by fatigue.

And so, in a real sense, Jesus was alone in the garden. As He prayed, His anguish deepened and became unbearable. He stood, and close to a stupor of fright at the visions He had seen, came back to the three, perhaps to seek human solace.

He looked down, and His heart

The exact location of the Garden of Gethsemane is unknown; however, scholars have determined that the garden was located in an olive grove on the Mount of Olives. The roots of the trees in this area may date back to the time of Jesus.
(Jeanne Conte)

ached as He saw the three sleeping. As Peter half opened his eyes, Jesus whispered: "Simon, are you sleeping? Were you not able to stay awake one hour? Keep awake and pray, all of you, that you may not succumb to temptation." He sighed. "The spirit is willing, but the flesh is weak."

Jesus went back to pray, now even further into the realm of agony than before. As He knelt again to tell His Father that He would accept the cup, the salty sweat, gleaming on His face and forehead, began to change color. It reddened and deepened in hue until, in His agony, He knew that it was blood.

THE BETRAYAL

FULTON OURSLER

THE BETRAYAL

Still, as of old
Man by himself is priced.
For thirty pieces Judas sold himself,
    not Christ.

–AUTHOR UNKNOWN

Judas waved back the guards while he leaned in and peered. Miraculously the darkness seemed to soften then, as if the stars grew brighter. With narrowing eyes Judas searched among gnarled and hunchbacked trees of immemorial age. But where were the eleven and the Master? Dimly, Judas began to make them out. That vast hunk of man sprawled on the grass, his head on a rolled-up cloak, was surely Peter, snoring. The slim form yonder by the pavilion platform was John, also deep in slumber. Other dark smudges under the trees were unrecognizable, but Judas counted eleven, all asleep. Their leader was invisible.

Judas would have entered then and brought the guards with him, but he was stopped by the sound of a familiar voice at prayer. He stood listening. Judas could hear the suffering voice: "My Father! If it be possible, let this cup pass from me! Nevertheless, not as I will, but as you will."

The silence after the prayer was touched by a low swishing sound as by a trailing garment brushing the grass. Out of the dark and walking by starlight the white figure of Jesus appeared, moving toward a sleeping disciple. Judas could see Him clearly now—tall, robed, walking barefoot across the chilly field. Jesus bent over the snoring man.

"It is enough, Peter. The hour has come," Jesus said simply. Peter scrambled to his feet and bared his knife.

Judas waited for no more. He laid a hard, damp hand on the wrist of the leader of the band, and whispered: "Now is the time. Let us go in and take Him. You will know Him sure—He will be the one I will kiss!"

The sound of rough voices and the clank of steel, the sight of the fires, brought all the drowsy disciples to their feet.

They blinked at the frightening torch-lit scene, shining with the cold brilliance of armor and swords.

Judas strode forward until he stood directly in front of Jesus.

"Hail, Master!"

Jesus moved toward Judas and seized him by the shoulders. Then the arms of Christ drew Judas to Him and the disciple kissed the Master on the cheek. At the signal, the Roman soldiers came forward, weapons in hand. But Jesus did not at once let Judas go. He held him tightly, His cheek laid against the tough ringlets, eyes lifted, as if asking a favor of the invisible. Then at last He released him, and as Judas stood back, the prisoner brought His hands together and held them out as He approached the Roman captain.

That was more than the panic-stricken Peter could bear. Peter sprang at the officer; there was a moment's tussle, a disorderly struggle, and then the ironic voice of Jesus:

"Peter, Peter, put up your sword!"

And Peter's fishing knife fell at his feet.

A soldier from the Temple scurried forward with a handful of ropes and began to tie the wrists of Jesus. That action was like a warning to the other disciples, who had been watching in startled dismay.

This sudden invasion of men in armor and others armed with cudgels and staves filled them with fright. The torches burned like small new worlds fuming in a dark universe. Voices rose in brawling question. Peter and all the others were overwhelmed with fear for their own safety. Stampeded, like wild creatures, they scampered off into the night. One, wrapped only in a linen cloth, was seized by a guard, but he tore himself free, leaving the garment in the soldier's hands; naked, he vanished among the trees. Leaping the hedges and running as fast as legs would carry them, they left Jesus, the captive, alone. ✸

THE LORD TURNED, AND LOOKED UPON PETER

The Saviour looked on Peter. Ay,
   no word,
No gesture of reproach! the heavens
   serene,
Though heavy with armed justice,
   did not lean
Their thunders that way!
   the forsaken Lord
Looked only on the traitor. None
   record
What that look was, none guess: for
   those who have seen
Wronged lovers loving through a
   death-pang keen,
Or pale-cheeked martyrs smiling to
   a sword,
Have missed Jehovah at the
   judgment-call.
And Peter, from the height of
   blasphemy—
"I never knew this man"—did quail
   and fall,
As knowing straight that God—and
   turned free
And went out speechless from the
   face of all,
And filled the silence,
   weeping bitterly.

—ELIZABETH BARRETT
BROWNING

THE INTERVIEW

PETER MARSHALL

The Roman Procurator, Pontius Pilate, was not in the best of moods. He did not relish having to rise at cockcrow to try a case.

Grimly, he gathered his purple-bordered toga over his arm and strode down the steps. The seething mass of humanity before him seemed centered around one solitary Man who was being thrust forward. Pilate's first impression was that He was perfectly harmless.

Many of the faces before him were livid. The crowd looked like a pack of snarling animals. The Roman governor raised his baton as a signal that the trial could begin and asked: "What accusation bring ye against this man?"

The reply was insolent. "If He were not an evil-doer we should not have delivered Him up to thee."

Once more Pilate looked at the prisoner. An evil-doer? If the Roman was any judge of men, and he prided himself on that, this prisoner was no vicious character.

"Take Him away," he said, turning to go back into the palace. "Take Him away and deal with Him according to your own law."

Now a veritable howl went up. "It is not lawful for us to put any man to death."

Ah, so that was what they wanted. The blood-lust was in their eyes. He knew now what the Jews wanted of him— to make convenience of his rank and position. But woe be to him if he blocked their intentions. Pilate hesitated. Once more his eyes rested on the prisoner.

His was the only calm face in that seething sea—and what a face it was! There was something in the eyes . . . in the set of the mouth . . . something about the bearing that was different, strange, compelling.

There came to the Roman governor an instinctive desire to get away from the crowd, to be alone with this Man and speak with Him face to face. So he turned and strode back into the palace and sat down upon the dais. Then he gave command that the prisoner be brought before him.

For a moment there was silence.

Then Pilate's involuntary question surprised even himself: "Art Thou the King of the Jews?"

A faint smile came over the face of Jesus. "Sayest thou this of thyself or did others tell it thee concerning Me?"

It was the first time that Pilate had heard the Man's voice. He did not say so, but it was the prisoner's deportment that had made him involuntarily associate kingliness with Him. "Am I a Jew?" he asked contemptuously. "Thine own nation and the chief priests have delivered Thee unto me. Tell me—what hast Thou done?"

What had He done? No crime certainly—no political misdemeanor. Had He not told John's messengers: "The blind receive their sight, and the lame walk, and the lepers are cleansed, and the deaf hear, and the dead are raised up, and the poor have the Gospel preached unto them."

That was something. But Pilate would not be interested in that.

So He said gently: "My kingdom is not of this world: if My kingdom were of this world, then would My servants fight, that I should not be delivered to the Jews: but now My kingdom is not from hence."

Pilate persisted: "Art Thou a king then?"

Here at any rate was no king whom Caesar need fear. "My kingdom is not of this world," Jesus had said.

His kingdom did not belong to the same order of things as Caesar's kingdom. Therefore, the two could never come into collision. His kingdom was a repudiation of all

PILATE'S WIFE'S DREAM

I see it all—I know the dusky sign—
A cross on Calvary, which Jews
    uprear
While Romans watch; and when the
    dawn shall shine,
Pilate, to judge the victim will appear,
Pass sentence—yield Him up
    to crucify;
And on that cross the spotless Christ
    must die.

What is this Hebrew Christ? To me
    unknown,
His lineage—doctrine—mission—yet
    how clear,
Is God-like goodness, in His
    actions shewn!
How straight and stainless is His
    life's career!
The ray of Deity that rests on Him,
In my eyes makes Olympian
    glory dim.

This day, time travails with a
    mighty birth,
This day, Truth stoops from heaven
    and visits earth,
Ere night descends, I shall more
    surely know
What guide to follow, in what path
    to go;
I wait in hope—I wait in solemn fear,
The oracle of God—
The sole, true God—to hear.

—CHARLOTTE BRONTË

And he released unto them him that for sedition and murder was cast into prison, whom they had desired; but he delivered Jesus to their will.

–LUKE 23:25

political aims. It was a flat denial of the insinuations made by the priests that the Nazarene was plotting treason.

But it was an assertion that claimed kingship of some sort. So Pilate probed further. "So Thou art a king then?"

And Jesus nodded. "Thou sayest. To this end have I been born, that I should bear witness unto the truth. Every one that is of the truth heareth My voice."

Pilate seemed a little weary of the interview. He had learned what he wanted to know—this man was harmless. "What is truth?" he asked.

Then, without waiting for a reply, he rose and went outside to give his answer to the impatient Jews. He held up his baton for silence. In a ringing voice he said: "I find no fault with this man."

The chief priests were now more angry than ever. They spat out their accusations. "He stirreth up the people. He teacheth throughout all Jewry, beginning from Galilee to this place."

The word "Galilee" leaped out at Pilate. He saw a possible loophole. "Is this man from Galilee?"

When the priests answered in the affirmative, he said firmly: "Then send the prisoner to Herod. I cannot try this case. It is not in my jurisdiction."

And Pilate thought that he had dismissed the matter, was well-rid of an embarrassing issue. The New Testament narratives leave no doubt that what Pilate most wanted was to find a way to release Christ.

But Christ before Herod was a greater enigma to the Jewish ruler than to the Roman. Herod expected to see Him do some tricks, for the stories of His miracles had long since been trickling into the court. The Jewish king was eager for a command performance.

But Jesus stood, silently eloquent. He had nothing to say—nothing, that is, to Herod. So Herod sent Him back to Pilate.

The howlings for His death now became even more vehement. And Pilate, supremely weary now of the whole matter, sat, chin in hand, on his curule chair—the cobalt-blue chair of judgment under the movable canopy—gloomily watching the yelling mob.

At that moment, a cohort bowed before him. "Sire, an urgent message." And he handed the Roman a thin wax tablet.

The Ecce Homo *arch rises over the narrow streets of Old Jerusalem in remembrance of Pilate's words upon his presentation of Jesus to the people.* Ecce Homo *means "Behold the Man!"* (Jeanne Conte)

It was a message from Pilate's wife, Claudia. Pilate frowned because never before had Claudia interrupted him in the midst of a hearing. Ordinarily, she would have not dared. The message was the more urgent for its brevity: "Have thou nothing to do with that just man: for I have suffered many things in a dream because of Him."

Pilate's thoughts went back to the night before . . . the nocturnal visit of the High Priest . . . Claudia had questioned him after the High Priest had left. Husband and wife had quarreled a bit. "It isn't really like you—a Roman—to agree to a man's death ahead of time. I have seen this man in the streets of Jerusalem, watched Him once for minutes on end from my litter. He seems harmless enough. I don't like this affair."

Pilate had slipped out that morning at cockcrow without waking Claudia. Now this—the Roman Procurator's hand trembled a bit. Dreams made him uneasy. Warnings could come that way. Perhaps Claudia was right after all.

SIMON THE CYRENE

KAHLIL GIBRAN

And as they came out, they found a man of Cyrene, Simon by name: him they compelled to bear His cross. And when they were come unto a place called Golgotha, that is to say, a place of a skull, They gave Him vinegar to drink mingled with gall: and when He had tasted thereof, He would not drink.

And they crucified Him, and parted His garments, casting lots: that it might be fulfilled which was spoken by the prophet, They parted My garments among them, and upon My vesture did they cast lots.
—MATTHEW 27:32–35

I was on my way to the fields when I saw Him carrying His cross; and multitudes were following Him.

Then I too walked beside Him.

His burden stopped Him many a time, for His body was exhausted.

Then a Roman soldier approached me, saying, "Come, you are strong and firm built; carry the cross of this man."

When I heard these words my heart swelled within me and I was grateful.

And I carried His cross.

It was heavy, for it was made of poplar soaked through with the rains of winter.

And Jesus looked at me. And the sweat of His forehead was running down upon His beard.

Again He looked at me and He said, "Do you too drink this? You shall indeed sip its rim with Me to the end of time."

So saying He placed His hand upon my free shoulder. And we walked together toward the Hill of the Skull.

But now I felt not the weight of the cross. I felt only His hand. And it was like the wing of a bird upon my shoulder.

(photo, opposite page)
The Via Dolorosa is traditionally believed to be the route taken by Jesus as He carried His cross from Pilate's palace to Calvary. (Jeff Greenberg/Unicorn)

SIMON OF CYRENE

I walked that day out to the death-marked hill—
They call the place "the skull"—and saw Him bear
His cross until He fell. It was not fair,
I thought, to place it on Him. Strength and skill
Were mine from country toil. I bore it till
We came to Golgotha. I did not dare
To speak my grief; I only thought to spare
Him pain—His grateful look lives with me still.

And as we walked along, some women wept.
I could not censure them—my eyes were dim.
But know ye what He said? His words I've kept
Within my heart these years for love of Him:
"Weep not for me. Dark days await you too.
Forgive these men: they know not what they do."

—GEORGIA HARKNESS

AT NOON

LEW WALLACE

And it was about the sixth hour, and there was a darkness over all the earth until the ninth hour. And the sun was darkened, and the veil of the Temple was rent in the midst. And when Jesus had cried with a loud voice, He said, Father, into Thy hands I commend My spirit: and having said thus, He gave up the ghost.

Now when the centurion saw what was done, he glorified God, saying, Certainly this was a righteous man.

–LUKE 23:44–47

The guard took the Nazarene's clothes from Him, so that He stood before the multitude naked. The stripes of the scourging He had received in the early morning were still bloody upon His back; yet He was laid pitilessly down, and stretched upon the cross. But not a groan, or cry, or word of remonstrance from the sufferer: nothing at which an enemy could laugh.

The workmen put their hands to the cross and carried it, burden and all, to the place of planting. At a word, they dropped the tree into the hole, and the body of the Nazarene also dropped heavily and hung by the bleeding hands. Still no cry of pain—only the divinest of all recorded exclamations, "Father, forgive them, for they know not what they do."

The cross, reared now above all other objects, and standing singly out against the sky, was greeted with a burst of delight; and all who could see and read the writing upon the board over the Nazarene's head made haste to decipher it. Soon as read, the legend was adopted and communicated, and presently the whole mighty concourse was ringing the salutation from side to side and repeating it with laughter, "King of the Jews! Hail, King of the Jews!"

The sun was rising rapidly to noon when suddenly a dimness began to fill the sky and cover the earth—at first no more than a scarce perceptible fading of the day; a twilight out of time; an evening gliding in upon the splendors of midday. But it deepened, and directly drew attention; whereat the noise of the shouting and laughter fell off, and men, doubting their senses, gazed at each other and turned pale.

The dimness went on deepening into obscurity, and that into positive darkness, but without deterring the bolder

(photo, opposite page)
Traces of the King's Game, a game often played by Roman soldiers as they taunted prisoners, can be seen on these stones. It is believed that these stones are within the area that was once Pilate's Palace. (Jeanne Conte)

spirits upon the knoll. One after the other the two thieves were raised on their crosses, and the crosses planted. The guard was then withdrawn, and the people set free closed in upon the height and surged up it, like a converging wave.

"Ha, ha! If Thou be King of the Jews, save Thyself," a soldier shouted.

Others wagged their heads wisely, saying, "He would destroy the Temple and rebuild it in three days, but cannot save Himself. If Thou be King of the Jews, or Son of God, come down," they said, loudly.

The breathing of the Nazarene grew harder; His sighs became great gasps. Only three hours upon the cross, and He was dying! A tremor shook the tortured body; there was a scream of fiercest anguish, and the mission and the earthly life were over at once. The heart, with all its love, was broken.

BENEATH THE SHADOW OF THE CROSS

Beneath the shadow of the cross,
　　As earthly hopes remove,
His new commandment Jesus gives,
　　His blessed word of Love.

O bond of union strong and deep!
　　O bond of perfect peace!
Not e'en the lifted cross can harm,
　　If we but hold to this.

Then, Jesus, be Thy Spirit ours!
　　And swift our feet shall move
To deeds of pure self-sacrifice,
　　And the sweet tasks of love.

—SAMUEL LONGFELLOW

129

THE SIGN ON THE CROSS

SIGMUND BROUWER

And Pilate wrote a title, and put it on the cross. And the writing was, JESUS OF NAZARETH THE KING OF THE JEWS.

This title then read many of the Jews: for the place where Jesus was crucified was nigh to the city: and it was written in Hebrew, and Greek, and Latin.

–JOHN 19:19–20

Only Pilate can explain why he instructed the sign to be worded as it was.

To be sure, it was customary for the charges against a criminal to be chalked in legible letters on a board. As the criminal bore his cross to the execution site, the board hung by a rope from the cross or was carried ahead by a herald.

Some might believe it was Pilate's intention to mock both Jesus and the troublesome Jews who had forced Pilate to declare the capital sentence. Yet Pilate had done his best to set Jesus free, and it seems more likely that if mockery was his goal, Pilate's target was simply the religious Jews so determined to kill Jesus.

Perhaps, instead, Jesus' simple words of truth and obvious innocence during the trial had touched Pilate enough that the hardened soldier actually felt Jesus deserved this dignity in His final hours.

Either way, the inscriptions stood—in Aramaic, Latin, and Greek.

Close readers of the Gospels will note that the inscription is worded slightly differently in each of the accounts. A reasonable explanation is that each Gospel writer chose a different inscription to translate. John, for example, gives us the Aramaic version—most Jews read this language, so it makes sense that the longest and most offensive inscription to them was written in Aramaic.

Aramaic, Latin, and Greek.

More significant than an explanation for discrepancies, however, is the witness given by the use of all three languages.

Latin was the official language of Rome.

Greek was most commonly used for communication

This mosaic of Jesus upon the cross hangs in the Church of the Holy Sepulchre.
(Jeanne Conte)

throughout the empire.

Aramaic reached the Jews of Israel.

The inscriptions, then, covered the intellectual, social, and religious spectrum of any who read the sign.

Yes, Pilate had his own reasons for posting the sign the way he did.

But God, who has purpose in everything, ensured that even this seemingly trivial detail worked to advance the kingdom for which Jesus gave His life. 🔲

THE CROSS AT THE CROSSWAYS

See There! God's signpost, standing at the ways
    Which every man of his free will must go—
Up the steep hill, or down the winding ways,
    One or the other, every man must go.

He forces no man, each must choose his way,
    And as he chooses so the end will be;
One went in front to point the Perfect Way,
    Who follows fears not where the end will be.

–JOHN OXENHAM

131

HIS FAITHFUL FOLLOWERS

ERMA FERRARI

And all His acquaintance, and the women that followed Him from Galilee, stood afar off, beholding these things. And, behold, there was a man named Joseph, a counsellor; and he was a good man, and a just: (The same had not consented to the counsel and deed of them;) he was of Arimathaea, a city of the Jews: who also himself waited for the kingdom of God. This man went unto Pilate, and begged the body of Jesus. And he took it down, and wrapped it in linen, and laid it in a sepulchre that was hewn in stone, wherein never man before was laid. And that day was the preparation, and the sabbath drew on.

–LUKE 23:49–54

The Jewish law forbade leaving a body upon a cross overnight. The body of Jesus must therefore be removed, but Pilate's consent was needed. Pilate had disapproved of the crucifixion of Jesus and would not want to be troubled further. Who had enough influence to approach the Roman governor again?

"What of Joseph of Arimathea?" somebody asked. Joseph was a member of the Sanhedrin, a righteous man who was looking for the kingdom of God, and Joseph had not consented to the death of Jesus. Joseph was willing to go to Pilate to ask for the body of the man in whose innocence he believed. Furthermore, he would bury the body in a tomb in which no man had yet lain, even though the law forbade giving an honorable burial to one whom the Sanhedrin had condemned to death.

Pilate gave his consent, and Joseph had the body of Jesus taken from the cross, wrapped in two pieces of fine linen, and buried in a new tomb, hewn out of a rock in a quiet garden not far from Joseph's home.

Certain women who had loved and ministered to Jesus were not content with this burial. The body of their Lord must be properly anointed. So they followed Joseph's men to learn where Jesus was to be buried. Then they hurried home to prepare the necessary spices and ointments before the Sabbath Day.

Before sundown they returned to anoint with gentle hands the body of their Lord. As they did so, a stranger entered the tomb. He, too, brought ointments and costly myrrh and aloes. The timid Nicodemus had come to anoint the body of Jesus. ✸

(photo, opposite page)
This stone may be similar to the one on which the body of Jesus was laid after He was taken from the cross. Here He would have been anointed with oils and spices in preparation for being placed in the tomb.
(Jeanne Conte)

HOLY SATURDAY

O Earth, who daily kissed His feet
Like lowly Magdalen—how sweet
(As oft His mother used) to keep
The silent watches of His sleep,
Till love demands the Prisoner,
And Death replies, "He is not here.

He passed my portal, where, afraid,
My footsteps faltered to invade
The region that beyond me lies:
Then, ere the dawn, I saw Him rise
In glory that dispelled my gloom
And made a Temple of the Tomb."

—JOHN BANISTER TABB

VII

SING HALLELUJAH

But thanks be to God, which

giveth us the victory through our

Lord Jesus Christ.

–1 CORINTHIANS 15:57

AN EMPTY TOMB

BONNELL SPENCER

*Now upon the first day of the
week, very early in the morning,
they came unto the sepulchre,
bringing the spices which they had
prepared, and certain others with
them. And they found the stone
rolled away from the sepulchre.
And they entered in, and found
not the body of the Lord Jesus.*

*And it came to pass, as they
were much perplexed there about,
behold, two men stood by them in
shining garments: And said unto
them, Why seek ye the living
among the dead? He is not here,
but is risen: remember how He
spake unto you when He was yet in
Galilee, Saying, The Son of man
must be delivered into the hands of
sinful men, and be crucified, and
the third day rise again. And they
remembered His words, and told
all these things unto the rest.*

—LUKE 24:1–9

*(photo, pages 134–135)
Sunrise on the western shore of the Sea of
Galilee. (Erich Lessing/Art Resource)*

The followers of our Lord also were confronted with the Empty Tomb. Very early on Sunday morning, a party of women set out from Jerusalem to visit the sepulchre. They had bought spices the evening before and were going to finish the anointing of the body, which they knew had been hurried and incomplete.

The two Marys had witnessed the interment. Joseph of Arimathea, a wealthy member of the Sanhedrin, had asked and obtained from Pilate permission to bury our Lord's body in his tomb on good Friday. Assisted by Nicodemus, a fellow-member of the Sanhedrin, and also, presumably, by a band of servants, Joseph had taken the body down from the cross, wrapped it in linen, and laid it in the sepulchre. The first three Gospels all seem to imply that Mary Magdalene and the other Mary had no share in the proceedings. This is understandable, since, as humble peasant women, they would have hesitated to intervene in a matter which was being directed by two of the chief men of Israel. They merely watched at a distance and saw where the body was laid.

Naturally, the holy women desired to minister in person to their Master's body and to complete with their own hands what had been done hastily by others. Yet they knew that it was dangerous to visit the tomb of One who had been put to death for insurrection.

There was another difficulty which they knew they must face. As they hurried on in the gray light of early dawn, they discussed it among themselves. "Who shall roll us away the stone from the door of the sepulchre?"

The stone must have been very great if four or more peasant women, accustomed as they were to heavy labor in

The National Shrine of Our Lady of Lourdes portrays the angels who kept watch outside the tomb of Jesus. (Jeanne Conte/courtesy of National Shrine of Our Lady of Lourdes)

EASTER

Rise, heart; thy Lord is risen. Sing
    His praise
      Without delays,
Who takes thee by the hand, that
    thou likewise
      With Him mayst rise:
That as His death calcined thee to
    dust,
His life may make thee gold, and
    much more, just.

Awake, my lute, and struggle for
    thy part
      With all thy art.
The cross taught all wood to
    resound His Name,
      Who bore the same.
His stretched sinews taught all
    strings what key
Is best to celebrate this most high
    day.

Consort both heart and lute, and
    twist a song
      Pleasant and long:
Or, since all music is but three
    parts vied
      And multiplied,
O let Thy blessed Spirit bear a part,
And make up our defects with His
    sweet art.

—GEORGE HERBERT

the house and field, feared they could not move it. It is the measure of their determination to render their final service to their dead Master that they set out to perform it knowing this obstacle lay across their path.

On entering the garden, they discovered that the anticipated difficulty had been removed. The stone was rolled away from the sepulchre. But this filled them more with dismay than with relief. Hastening across the intervening space, they peered breathlessly into the semidarkness. Their worst fears were realized. Transfixed with grief, they dropped the now useless spices on the ground. The tomb was empty.

We must make an effort of imagination to enter into their experience at that moment. We know the tomb was empty because Christ had risen from the dead. Its very emptiness starts us shouting, "Alleluia!" To the holy women, it brought no such message of joy. "For as yet they knew not the scripture, that He must rise again from the dead." To them, it was the ultimate horror—a robbed grave.

Even that poor broken body which had been taken

Many believe the garden tomb in the Garden of Joseph of Arimathea to be the actual tomb of Christ. The trough in front of the tomb was used to guide the massive rolling stone in front of the opening. (R. Opfer/H. Armstrong Roberts)

down from the cross had not been allowed to rest in the tomb. It was the culminating desecration. The last object on which they might have lavished their heartbroken ministrations had been taken from them. As thoughts such as these filled their minds, their cup of sorrow overflowed in a grief "too deep for tears."

After a moment of frozen stupor, one of the women broke from the group and rushed from the garden. This would seem to be the only way to reconcile the discrepancy in our accounts of the episode. For in the first three Gospels, the discovery of the Empty Tomb is followed at once by the appearance of the angel (Saint Luke says two angels) with the message that Christ is risen. Yet the Fourth Gospel asserts definitely that Mary Magdalene alone brought word of the Empty Tomb to Peter and John, and that she made no mention of any angelic message. Since she would hardly have failed to speak of this had she heard it, we are forced to conclude that she left before the angel was seen.

Two little phrases in the variant accounts point in the same direction. Both Saint Mark and Saint Luke state explicitly that it was after the women had entered "into the sepulchre" that the angel was discovered. Saint John, on the other hand, says, "Mary Magdalene . . . seeth the stone taken away from the sepulchre. Then she runneth, and cometh to Simon Peter." One glimpse into the Empty Tomb is enough to start the impetuous Magdalene off for the disciples. It is characteristic of Saint John thus to correct the earlier accounts without specifically contradicting them.

After Mary Magdalene left, the other women recovered sufficiently from their initial shock to investigate further. Then they saw the angel and heard his message: "Ye seek Jesus of Nazareth, which was crucified: He is risen; He is not here: behold the place where they laid Him. But go your way, tell His disciples and Peter that He goeth before you into Galilee: there shall ye see Him, as He said unto you."

Encouraging as the angel's words sound to us, who know the full truth of the Resurrection, they could hardly have been so to the holy women. The vision of an angel was in itself a terrifying experience. His message, so completely unexpected, must have been almost unintelligible to them. They could not absorb or understand its meaning. Probably if it conveyed anything to them at all, it gave them a vague and uneasy impression that somehow the Lord was alive. Far from removing the terror which the discovery of the Empty Tomb had impressed upon them, it greatly increased it. They fled from the sepulchre in amazement and fear.

Meanwhile, Mary Magdalene reached Peter and John. "They have taken away the Lord out of the sepulchre, and we know not where they have laid Him." At once the disciples set out for the garden, with Mary Magdalene following them. Apparently, taking a slightly different route through the crooked little streets of the city, they missed the party of women who were returning. They reached the sepulchre and found it as Mary Magdalene had described it. No angel appeared. Without any mitigation, they were made to face the Empty Tomb. ◉

MARY MAGDALENE

At dawn she sought the
    Savior slain,
To kiss the spot where
    He had lain
And weep warm tears, like
    springtime rain;

When lo, there stood, unstained
    of death,
A man that spoke with low sweet
    breath;
And "Master!" Mary answereth.

From out the far and fragrant years
How sweeter than the songs of seers
That tender offering of tears!

—RICHARD BURTON

And when she had thus said, she turned herself back, and saw Jesus standing, and knew not that it was Jesus.

–JOHN 20:14

MARY MAGDALENE MEETS THE RISEN LORD

PETER MARSHALL

But Mary Magdalene, still weeping, lingered at the edge of the garden.

Along with the other women, she had come to find a dead body and had been shocked to find the grave empty. She thought it had been broken open—grave-robbers perhaps. She did not know. She could not think clearly. Only one thought seems to have absorbed her soul—the body of the Lord had been lost; she must find Him!

She ran as never before back toward the empty tomb, with the speed and unawareness of time and distance that grief or fear or love can impart.

"But Mary stood without at the sepulchre weeping; and as she wept, she stooped down and looked into the sepulchre, and she turned herself back and saw Jesus standing, and knew not that it was Jesus.

"Jesus saith unto her: 'Woman, why weepest thou? Whom seekest thou?'"

And John tells us that she thought He was the gardener. She fell at His feet, her eyes brimming with tears—her head down—sobbing, "Sir, if thou hast taken Him hence, tell me where thou hast laid Him, and I will take Him away."

To her tortured mind there was a gleam of hope that perhaps the gardener, for some reason known only to him, had moved the body. She was red-eyed. She had not slept since Friday. There had been no taste for food. She had been living on grief and bereaved love.

"Jesus saith unto her, 'Mary.'"

His voice startled her. She would have recognized it

anywhere.

She lifted her head with a jerk, blinked back the tears from her eyes, and looked—right into His eyes.

She knew—her heart told her first and then her mind. She saw the livid marks of the nails in His hands; and looking up into His face, she whispered: "Rabboni!"

The loveliest music of that first Easter dawn is the sound of those words echoing in the Garden. His gentle "Mary" and her breathless "Master!"

Mary had come prepared to weep—now she could worship. She had come expecting to see Him lying in the tomb. She had found Him walking in the newness of resurrected life. ▨

Bougainvillea *is one of many plant species that adds color to the often arid landscape of Israel.* (Jeanne Conte)

EASTER PRAYER

Oh, let me know
The power of Thy resurrection!
Oh, let me show
Thy risen life in clear reflection!
Oh, let me soar
Where Thou, my Saviour Christ, art gone before!
In mind and heart
Let me dwell always, only, where Thou art.

Oh, let me give
Out of the gifts Thou freely givest;
Oh, let me live
With life abundantly because Thou livest;

Oh, make me shine
In darkest places, for Thy light is mine;
Oh, let me be
A faithful witness for Thy truth and Thee.

Oh, let me show
The strong reality of gospel story;
Oh, let me go
From strength to strength, from glory unto glory;
Oh, let me sing
For very joy, because Thou art my King;
Oh, let me praise
Thy love and faithfulness through all my days.

—FRANCES RIDLEY HAVERGAL

A STRANGER WALKS TO EMMAUS

ELIZABETH STUART PHELPS

And, behold, two of them went that same day to a village called Emmaus, which was from Jerusalem about threescore furlongs. And they talked together of all these things which had happened. And it came to pass, that, while they communed together and reasoned, Jesus Himself drew near, and went with them.

–LUKE 24:13–15

It was late afternoon of the first Easter when two [men], restless with sorrow, went for a walk to a place called Emmaus. Their hearts were as heavy as the clods of the grave. Their Lord was dead.

In the bewilderment of fresh bereavement, they talked drearily—of all that was precious and all that was confusing in His history; of the failure of His purposes, of the ruin of their hopes and of His.

A stranger joined them as they were walking and entered into their conversation. They thought him a very ignorant man, though he had not that appearance, for he questioned them minutely about the life and death of their rabbi. Was there a foreigner in Jerusalem who had not heard what had happened? They answered him with a sort of surprised condescension, but they readily began to talk about their Lord; indeed, they could not speak of anything else.

But as they strolled and talked, their feeling about the stranger underwent one of the swift transformations which simple minds experience in the presence of a superior. This was no ordinary tourist. This was a master of knowledge. He spoke of the Hebrew Messiah, of the meaning of ancient prophetic poetry, of the possibilities hidden in the scriptures. He spoke of the recent events that had shaken Palestine—of the national hopes and of the national shame.

The two disciples felt deeply drawn to the stranger; their thoughts took a high turn. Courage and faith swept back upon their despairing hearts like fire from heaven upon an abandoned altar. They clung so to the stranger that, when he

would have left them, they begged him to accept their hospitality. So he indulged them, smiling, and went to supper with them in their simple house. There it seemed the only right thing for him to do was to take the head of the table and serve; his hosts did not even wonder why. And it seemed to be wholly expected that he should ask the blessing of God upon the bread. Then—it seemed not strange, in any way, when the two began slowly and quietly to understand who He was. And they who loved and mourned a dead Christ lifted their eyes and perceived that He was alive. ✻

It was along the road to Emmaus, pictured at right, that Jesus appeared to two of His followers after His death and resurrection. They did not recognize Him at first. (Jeanne Conte)

FEED MY SHEEP

FULTON SHEEN

This is now the third time that
Jesus showed Himself to His
disciples, after that He was risen
from the dead.

–JOHN 21:14

LOVEST THOU ME?

A group had gathered
    on the shore that bounds
The restless waters of Tiberias.
The weary fishermen,
    who, all night long,
Had cast their nets in vain,
    now saw amazed
The wondrous product of
    their later toil,
And, half in terror, cried—
    "It is the Lord!"
And He—mysterious Man!—
    whom late they saw
Expire in agony upon the cross,
Stood calmly in their midst
    and hushed their fear.

Impetuous Peter,
    bolder than the rest,
Had met his Master first
    and sought to prove
His zealous confidence
    and greater love.
Him loving, yet reproving
    for his warmth,
The Lord addressed: "Thou son of
    Jonas, hear!
And answer truly if thou lovest Me?"

After the events of the Passover week in Jerusalem, the Apostles returned again to their former haunts and abodes, and particularly to the Sea of Galilee so full of tender memories. It was while they were fishing that the Lord had called them to be "Fishers of Men." Galilee would now be the scene of the Lord's last miracle, as it was the scene of His first. On the first occasion, there was "no wine"; on this last occasion there were "no fish."

Peter, taking the leadership and giving the inspiration to others, said: "I am going out fishing."

"We will go with you," said the others.

Though they had labored all the night, they caught nothing. When morning came they saw Our Lord on the shore, but they did not know that it was He. This was the third time that He came near to them as One Unknown in order to draw out their affections. Though they were near enough to the shore to address Him, like the disciples at Emmaus they neither discerned His Person nor recognized His voice, so enveloped was the Risen Body with glory. He was on the shore and they were on the sea. Our Lord spoke to them, saying: "Friends, have you caught anything?"

They answered, "No."

He said, "Shoot the net to starboard, and you will make a catch."

The Apostles must have remembered another such command when Our Lord told them to let down their nets for a draught, not specifying right or left. Then Our Lord was in the boat; now He was on the shore. The tossings of life were over. Immediately, in obedience to the Divine command, they were so successful in their catch that they were unable to draw the nets because of the multitude of fishes. In this miraculous draught of fishes they were made strong; for immediately John said to Peter: "It is the Lord!"

Once before, when Our Savior had walked on the waves toward the ship, Peter could not wait for the Master to come to him, so he asked the Master to bid him come upon the water. Now he swam to shore after girding himself out of reverence for His Savior.

The other six remained in the boat. When they came to shore, they saw fire, fish laid thereon, and some bread, which the compassionate Savior had prepared for them. The Son of God was preparing a meal for His poor fishermen. After they had dragged the net ashore and counted the one hundred and fifty-three fish they had caught, they were well convinced that it was the Lord.

The following scene took place after they had dined. As He gave the Eucharist after the supper and the power to forgive sins after He had eaten with them, so now, after partaking of bread and fish, He turned to the one who had denied Him three times and asked a triple affirmation of love. The confession of love must precede the bestowing of authority; authority without love is tyranny. "Simon, son of John, do you love Me more than all else?"

Peter was now addressed as Simon, son of John, Simon being his original name. Our Lord thus reminded Peter of his past as a natural man, but especially of his fall or denial. He had been living by nature rather than grace. The title also had another significance; it must have reminded Peter of his glorious confession when Our Lord said to him, "Blessed art thou Simon, son of John," and made him the rock on which He would build His church.

In answer to the question about love, Peter said: "Yes, Lord, You know that I love You."

"Then feed My lambs," He said.

Thrice fell this question
  on his anxious ear,
While wonder first, and then
  dismay and grief,
Oppressed him as his answer
  thus he made—
"Yea, Lord, Thou knowest that
  I love Thee well."

"Then *feed My lambs,*" the
  Holy Shepherd said:
"If Me thou lovest more
  than all beside,
Then, *feed my lambs!* If thou
  wilt prove thy zeal,
And thus insure thy
  Master's welcome praise,
Go *feed My lambs!* I ask
  no arduous toil—
No deed of high emprise
  thy powers shall task,
I only bid thee *feed my lambs!*"
  He said,
And soon for heav'n departed,
  there to watch
His under-shepherds while they
guard His flock.

O ye, whose holy privilege it is
To serve Him thus, see that
  ye *feed His lambs!*
So shall ye gain the
  evidence ye seek,
That your commission bears
  His sacred seal:
So shall ye prove your love—
  and so acquire
The rich reward on which your
hopes are fixed.

—JULIAN CRAMER

THOMAS BELIEVES

WILLIAM BARCLAY

Thomas is best remembered as the man who could not believe. When Jesus had died upon the cross, and when it seemed that the end had finally come, Thomas's only desire was to be alone. So it happened that when Jesus came back to the disciples, Thomas was not there and utterly refused to believe the good news. He said that he would not believe unless he actually saw and touched and handled the nail-prints in Jesus' hands and the gash of the spear in His side. Thomas had to see before he would believe.

Ultimately, Thomas became a man of devotion and of faith. Jesus came back. He invited Thomas to put his finger in the nail-prints and his hand in His side. And confronted with the risen Lord, Thomas breathed out the greatest confession of faith in the New Testament: "My Lord and my God."

Two outstanding facts emerge from the story of Thomas. The first truth is that Jesus blames no man for wanting to be sure. Jesus did not blame Thomas for his doubts; Jesus knew that once Thomas had fought his way through the wilderness of his doubts he would be the surest man in Christendom. Jesus never says to a man: "You must have no doubts." Rather He says: "You must never profess a faith of which you are not absolutely sure, and you must fight your battle until you reach your certainty." But it must be noted that certainty came to Thomas, not through intellectual conviction of the truth of a creed, but through first-hand experience of the power and the presence of Jesus Christ. Thomas became sure, not of things about Jesus Christ, but of Jesus Christ Himself.

The second truth is that certainty is most likely to come to a man in the fellowship of believers. When Thomas was alone, he was doubly alone. By cutting himself off from the fellowship of men, Thomas had also cut himself off from Jesus Christ; and it was when he came back into that fellowship that he met Christ again. That is not to say that a man cannot find Jesus Christ in the solitude and the silence; but it is to say that nowhere is a man more likely to find Christ than in the company of those who love Christ.

Jesus appeared to His disciples numerous times in various places following His death and resurrection—including appearances by the Sea of Galilee, pictured below. (Erich Lessing/Art Resource)

PRAYER OF A MODERN THOMAS

If Thou, O God, the Christ didst leave,
In Him, not Thee, I do believe;
  To Jesus dying, all alone,
  To His dark Cross not Thy bright Throne,
My hopeless hands will cleave.

But if it was Thy love that died,
Thy voice that in the darkness cried,
  The print of nails I long to see,
  In Thy hands, God, who fashioned me,
Show me *Thy* piercèd side.

—EDWARD SHILLITO

RETURN TO THE FATHER

GEORGE HODGES

Jesus saith unto her, Touch Me not; for I am not yet ascended to My Father: but go to My brethren, and say unto them, I ascend unto My Father, and your Father; and to My God, and your God.

–JOHN 20:17

So forty days passed by. Some of them were days of wonder, when the Lord came and talked with the disciples. Others were days of expectation, when the disciples waited and He did not come. Indeed, they knew not at what moment or in what place He might appear.

One purpose of these appearances was to make them certain that He who had died upon the cross had come to life again. They saw Him face to face and heard Him speak. Thus they knew beyond all doubt that He was indeed the Son of God. He was the Word of God; that is, by Him God spoke. And the Word was God. In Him, their friend, God dwelt here on earth. They had not understood it. When His enemies had seized Him, His disciples had forsaken Him and fled. But now, seeing that death had no dominion over Him, they cried with Thomas, "My Lord and my God."

Another purpose of the appearances was to assure them that death is not the end. Christ came back, declaring that death is not a wall but a door. After we die we shall live again; He said, "Because I live, ye shall live also."

Then He gave His disciples their last instructions. They were to go now and teach what He had taught them. What they had heard in secret, they were to proclaim openly. Those who received the teaching and believed, and desired to live in the new way, they were to baptize. Thus they were to initiate them into a new society. He had already told them how they were to break bread and eat it, and to pour wine and drink it, in remembrance of Him. This they were to do at the meetings of the new society.

One matter which still perplexed them. The kingdom of God which they had so long expected, and of which the Lord had said so much, when and how was it to come? Even now they could not get rid of the old notion of a kingdom with a palace and a throne and a place of power. So they asked, "Lord, wilt Thou at this time restore again the kingdom to Israel?" And He answered, "The time is in the hand of the Father, and it is not for you to know it. But the kingdom is in your own hearts and in the hearts of those who shall receive your words. You shall be the founders of it. You who today are poor, and unknown in the great world, and hated by many men, shall be given power from on high, the power of goodness, and of love, and of the grace of God. You shall be witnesses unto Me, telling how I came, the Son of God, from heaven, to give men life here and hereafter, teaching them to live as I have commanded you, showing My spirit in your lives. And lo, I am with you always, even unto the end of the world."

When He had spoken these things, raising His hands over His disciples in farewell and blessing, while they beheld, He was taken up, and a cloud received Him out of their sight. And while they looked steadfastly toward heaven, as He went up, behold, two men stood by them in white apparel, saying, "Ye men of Galilee, why stand ye gazing up into heaven? This same Jesus which is taken up from you into heaven shall so come in like manner as ye have seen Him go into heaven." And the disciples remembered the saying, "A little while, and ye shall not see Me; and again, a little while, and ye shall see Me, because I go to the Father." They began to understand it. They began to see that the Lord had appeared and disappeared during the forty days to teach them to expect Him always and everywhere.

Into the cloud He went, and out of the cloud He comes, the cloud of human need. They fell upon their faces and worshiped the King of Glory. Their hearts were full of faith and love and joy. He had gone away and out of sight only to return invisible and to abide with them and with us all forever. ❂

ASCENSION HYMN

A hymn of glory let us sing;
New songs throughout the world
   shall ring;
By a new way none ever trod
Christ mounteth to the throne
   of God.

The apostles on the mountain stand,
The mystic mount, in Holy Land;
They, with the Virgin Mother, see
Jesus ascend in majesty.

The angels say to the eleven:
"Why stand ye gazing into heaven?
This is the Saviour—this is He!
Jesus hath triumphed gloriously!"

They said the Lord should
   come again,
As these beheld Him rising then,
Calm soaring through the
   radiant sky,
Mounting its dazzling summits high.

May our affections thither tend,
And thither constantly ascend,
Where, seated on the Father's throne,
Thee reigning in the heavens
   we own!

Be Thou our present joy, O Lord!
Who wilt be ever our reward;
And, as the countless ages flee,
May all our glory be in Thee!

—THE VENERABLE BEDE

VIII

EPILOGUE

For God sent not His Son into the world to condemn the world; but that the world through Him might be saved.

–JOHN 3:17

MORE THAN A TEACHER

FULTON SHEEN

Then the eleven disciples went away into Galilee, into a mountain where Jesus had appointed them. And when they saw Him, they worshiped Him: but some doubted. And Jesus came and spake unto them, saying, All power is given unto Me in heaven and in earth. Go ye therefore, and teach all nations, baptizing them in the name of the Father, and of the Son, and of the Holy Ghost: Teaching them to observe all things whatsoever I have commanded you: and, lo, I am with you always, even unto the end of the world. Amen.

—MATTHEW 28:16-20

(photo, pages 150–151)
The region once known as Judea includes four different land types: coastal plains, lowlands, hill country, and desert. It was in Bethlehem of Judea that Jesus was born and in Jerusalem of Judea that He was crucified.
(Starfoto/Zefa/H. Armstrong Roberts)

Great teachers give instructions to their disciples, but has any teacher ever made his death the pattern of theirs? Even when [Jesus] acted as a Teacher, He made the Cross to cast its shadow over His Apostles. The sufferings they would endure would be identical to what He would endure. He had been called the Lamb of God who would be sacrificed for the sins of the world; and since they were identified with Him, He warned them of their fate: "Look, I send you out like sheep among wolves."

As He had no illusions about what the world would do to Him, so He had no illusions about those who would be linked closest to Him as branches to the vine. No sage or mystic, no Buddha or Confucius has ever believed that his teaching would so awaken the antagonism of men as to bring about his violent death; but more important still, no human teacher has ever believed that his disciples would suffer a similar fate, just because they were his disciples.

The Apostles were not yet persecuted, nor were they annoyed very much before the Crucifixion and Pentecost. But He told them the kind of treatment they were to expect of men later on. Hardly prepared for what would happen to Him, how could they even faintly imagine what would happen to themselves?

Foretelling, without telling how, that He would be betrayed by one who was so close to Him, He gave them a better view of the Cross by telling them that betrayers will be of their own household, that brothers will betray brothers: "All will hate you for your allegiance to Me."

At this point in His discourse to the Apostles, He made clear that since He came to die and not live, so they must be prepared to die and not live. If the world gave Him a Cross, then they must expect one; if the world would say He had a devil, they could expect to be called "devils."

There would be a vindication for the wrong done them, and all the hidden things would be revealed.

Next, the Apostles were forewarned that those who accepted Him would be hated by the members of their own families. The Gospel would stir up strife between those who would accept Him and those who would reject Him. But they were not to think that all this was a loss. There is a double life: the physical and the spiritual. Tertullian noted that when the Romans put the early Christians to death, the pagan appeal always was: "Save your life; do not throw your life away." But as He would lay down His life and take it up again, so too what they would lose biologically, they would save spiritually: "By gaining his life a man will lose it; by losing his life for My sake, he will gain it."

That the Cross was the crowning incident in His life, the primary reason for His coming, is evident once again as He invited them to Crucifixion. It is unthinkable that He would urge them to a ransoming death unless He Himself had willed it for Himself as the Lamb slain from the beginning of the world. Later on, Peter and Andrew would understand what He meant that day, when they too would be crucified.

Immediately after Pentecost, when Christ sent His Spirit upon the Apostles, the full meaning of the Crucifixion dawned on Peter, and he summarized what he heard in the pre-Calvary instructions of Our Lord: "You used heathen men to crucify and kill Him. But God raised Him to life again, setting Him free from the pangs of death, because it could not be that death should keep Him in its grip."

The Cross was no accident in His life; it would be none in theirs or His followers' either. ✖

THE GOOD COMPANION

Wayworn and weary,
    With feet stone-bruised
        and soiled,
He walked the dusty ways
    Of all the men who toiled.

Men who tilled the prairie
    And turned the teeming sod
Knew as they turned the furrow
    They walked and wrought
        with God.

The weary, heavy-laden,
    The humble toiling folk,
Knew who will lift the burden;
    He feels and shares their yoke.

The stony way He traveled
    Led to Calvary's stark hill,
But He walked with John and Peter,
    Knowing man's sorrows still.

The long, long way to Calvary
    His earthly footsteps led,
But John and Peter afterward
    Remembered what He said.

—BELLE F. OWENS

A PORTRAIT OF JESUS

HENRI DANIEL-ROPS

Perhaps we should now try to draw a portrait of the Man whom, so far, we have tried to discover through the record of what He said and did.

It is obvious as we read the Gospels that Jesus was a plain man, and that He lived among the humble folk, from whom His disciples were drawn, as one of themselves. It is not, however, historically accurate to go to extremes and rank Him among the lowest classes. Jesus had many traits in common with the crowds who followed Him.

His clothing can hardly have differed much from that still worn by peasants. He would wear a linen tunic in all weather, adding a woolen cloak in the winter and this, as prescribed by the Law, would have blue tassels, these forming the "hem of His cloak" which the woman with a hemorrhage touched, and was cured. When He prayed, He would perhaps put on the ritual white cloak with purple bands.

When He went on a journey He would, quite naturally, expect hospitality and shelter wherever He happened to be. This was the traditional custom and, to a large extent, it still exists. A straw mattress, or a sort of string hammock, or even a rug or mat would be laid out in one of the rooms of the house, or on a balcony or terrace, for the climate is favorable to sleeping out of doors.

Jesus depended largely on hospitality for food and shelter. The Twelve certainly had a common purse and, according to John, it was kept by Judas. They had rich friends, mostly women, who "ministered to Him with the means they had." But it was not very luxurious living. The Galilean peasant ate bread, milk products, fruit and vegetables and, naturally, fish.

There has been a great deal of debate as to what languages Jesus spoke. At the time He lived, as for some two centuries previously, the vernacular was Aramaic.

It is certain, however, that Aramaic was not the only language He spoke. Luke tells us how, when He came to Nazareth, "where He had been brought up; He went into the synagogue there, as His custom was, on the Sabbath day, and stood up to read." He must therefore have read Hebrew, which, although it had been displaced by Aramaic as the vernacular tongue since the fourth century B.C., had survived as the liturgical language.

Did Jesus speak it [Greek]? There is nothing in the Gospel record, no trace of Hellenic style, to suggest that He did. Yet the dialogue between Jesus and Pilate, so forceful and direct, does not give the impression that it was conducted by means of an interpreter.

The personality of Jesus is not only manifestly sincere, it is unshakable. You cannot doubt that here is a master of the event. He is never deflected from what He wishes to do either by the applause of crowds or by checks and opposition. If He adapts Himself to circumstances and submits to affronts without protest, it is biding His own good time. He never capitulates and never hesitates or weakens before the machinations of His enemies.

The perfection of the human character of Jesus lies in the union and the balance of these three qualities: sincerity, firmness, and authority. In truth, in Him divinity was ever and always present. The greatest saints have trembled in awe at the very thought of God; Jesus did not, for He was equal with the Father. We cannot say of Him, who is the Alpha and Omega of all mystical endeavor, that He is Himself a mystic. Once more as in all our attempts to draw a portrait of Jesus we catch a glimpse of the mystery of the Godhead behind the human face.

IS THIS THE FACE?

Is this the face that thrills with awe
Seraphs who veil their face above?
Is this the face without a flaw
    The face that is the face of love?
Yea, this defaced, a lifeless clod,
    Hath all creation's love sufficed,
Hath satisfied the love of God,
    This face the face of Jesus Christ.

—CHRISTINA ROSSETTI

PREACHING THE GOSPEL

BONNELL SPENCER

These words are the climax and theme of the first Christian sermon, which Peter addressed to the crowd on [Pentecost] morning. Clearly, he believed the Resurrection of Christ to be the keynote of the Gospel. He singled it out for primary emphasis and counted on it to convince others, as it had already convinced him, that Jesus was "both Lord and Christ." Nor was he disappointed. Many in the crowd responded to his sermon by asking the Apostles, "Men and brethren, what shall we do?" and about three thousand received baptism on that same day.

The Apostles considered that the characteristic function of their office was to give eyewitness testimony to the Resurrection of Christ. When, ten days earlier, Peter had asked the others to choose a man to "take part of this ministry and apostleship, from which Judas by transgression fell," they selected Joseph and Matthias, who had been with Jesus "unto that same day that He was taken up," that is, until the Ascension. They were eligible because they had seen the Risen Christ. Matthias was chosen by lot and "ordained to be a witness of (Christ's) Resurrection."

We can easily understand why that event loomed so large in the Apostles' thought. It had transformed their lives and made the preaching of the Gospel possible. On Holy Saturday, they had been the victims of grief-stricken fear. On Easter, all was changed. Death had not ended their association with Him. It had raised it to a higher, more glorious, more intimate plane. Wonderful as His friendship in Galilee had been, it took on a new significance now that He had risen from the grave. Forty days of intermittent Resurrection appearances convinced them that Christ's work on earth, far

from being finished, was just beginning. The termination of the
appearances with the Ascension did
not plunge them into grief. They
understood enough by then to realize that, although they would see
His face on earth no more, He was
not leaving them. On [Pentecost],
they received the Holy Spirit and
began forthwith to proclaim the
Good News that God had raised
Jesus from the dead.

The Resurrection also gave
them a Gospel to preach. Without
that experience, they would have
been able to tell men only of the
tragedy which had occurred on
Calvary. Had this been the end of
the story, it would have indicated
that God's final effort to save man
had failed. God Himself could not
overcome such impenitence and
hardness of heart. Man had had and had lost his last chance.
The Christian message would have been one of despair.

*This ancient baptismal font, beautifully
carved from stone, was unearthed not far
from the Sea of Galilee.* (Jeanne Conte)

The Resurrection was Christ's vindication. It revealed
His triumph over sin and death. He had not been defeated
and killed. He had laid down His life for the world. Now
He had taken it up again that He might reap the harvest
His sacrifice had won. At last, the disciples were able to
understand His purpose. They recognized who He was. He
was not only the Messiah. He was the Lamb of God that
taketh away the sins of the world. He was the Lord of life
and of death. Hardly daring to believe, they fell on their
knees and worshiped Him as God. ▨

ONE SOLITARY LIFE

He was born in an obscure village, the child of a peasant woman. He worked in a carpentry shop until He was thirty, and then for three years He was an itinerant preacher.

When the tide of popular opinion turned against Him, His friends ran away. He was turned over to His enemies. He was tried and convicted. He was nailed upon a cross between two thieves. When He was dead, He was laid in a borrowed grave.

He never wrote a book. He never held an office. He never owned a home. He never went to college. He never traveled more than two hundred miles from the place where He was born. He never did one of the things that usually accompanies greatness.

Yet all the armies that ever marched, and all the governments that ever sat, and all the kings that ever reigned, have not affected life upon this earth as powerfully as has that One Solitary Life. ✸

—AUTHOR UNKNOWN

Slopes of the Mount of Olives, near the Valley of Kidron. (R. Opfer/H. Armstrong Roberts)

Author Index

Title Index

SUBJECT INDEX